Harry & Meghan

The Wedding Album

BY ROBERT JOBSON

Printed in the UK by CPI Colour on 130g Chorus Silk.
This paper has been independently certified according to
the standards of the Forest Stewardship Council® (FSC)®.

978-1-906670-62-7

His Royal Highness The Prince of Wales, K.G., K.T.
requests the pleasure of the company of

at the Marriage of
His Royal Highness Prince Henry of Wales
with
Ms Meghan Markle
at St. George's Chapel, Windsor Castle
on Saturday, 19th May, 2018 at 12 Noon
followed by a Reception at Windsor Castle

Dress:

A reply is requested to
Assistant Comptroller, Lord Chamberlain's Office,
Buckingham Palace, London SW1A 1AA
www.rsvplord p... p... ...k

INTRODUCTION

BY ROBERT JOBSON

The genius of a royal wedding lies in the combination of its simplicity, its invocation of history and its sense of splendour. It lies, too, in its ability to appeal to people on a personal level, as well as being a sensational, almost magical, visual spectacle. The build-up to the wedding of Prince Henry of Wales – now sixth in line to the British throne and known popularly as Prince Harry – and his American bride Ms Rachel Meghan Markle certainly captured the popular imagination.

Celebrated by close friends, family and dedicated royal fans in Windsor, it was enthusiastically cheered across the country, the Commonwealth and the rest of the world.

This royal wedding – watched by a global television audience of some two billion – as well as being a celebration of love, will have bolstered Britain's coffers by an estimated £500 million, experts claim.

Harry and Meghan's love story has also given the Royal Family's popularity a huge boost. Not since the days of the late Diana, Princess of Wales, has there been this degree of interest from young people in the Royal Family and the new "princess" who has married into it.

Harry, who I've watched grow up while chronicling the Windsor story for more than 25 years, has developed from a mischievous young man into the more mature version of himself we see now. Today, he is a prince who takes his public duties and charity responsibilities very seriously – even if he doesn't appear to take himself too seriously.

In his choice of wife – the beautiful, biracial, divorced actress Meghan – he has once again shown the determination to live his life his way and on his terms. When he met Meghan, he said the "stars were aligned". She was "the one" and he said he knew that he would have to "raise his game" to woo her. Their modern-day love story may not be the stuff of fairy tales, but it is an enchanting love story of our times.

This book, published by SJH Publishing, is a celebration in photographs and words of Harry and Meghan's love story. Using the brilliant images of my friend Robin Nunn – whose firm Nunn Syndication is the world's largest independently owned specialist royal photographic image source – the book captures the very essence of these two people as it documents their journey together and their historic union.

Harry is truly a prince for our times. Together with Meghan he has helped the Royal Family show itself to be much more in touch with the public it serves. And his princely marriage has the power to unite us all.

I am sure you will want to join me in raising a glass and wishing the Duke and Duchess of Sussex all the happiness in the world on their future life together.

CONTENTS

Chapter One

THE WEDDING

The union of Harry and Meghan
was a truly unique transatlantic
celebration – even if the royal couple
were trying to keep the occasion relatively
low key – that included a host of
personal touches from the glamorous
bride and groom

It had all the hallmarks of the grand finalé of a Hollywood love story, only this romantic tale starred a real-life prince, Henry of Wales, and his beautiful actress Meghan Markle.

And, like a Hollywood love story, this showpiece wedding attracted an audience of millions from around the world. Imbued with centuries-old tradition, it featured British pomp and pageantry at its finest, all staged in the majestic St George's Chapel in the grounds of the historic Windsor Castle.

Meghan arrived in a rare Rolls-Royce – a Phantom IV, the first of only 18 built, and one presented to the newlyweds Princess Elizabeth and the Duke of Edinburgh in 1950. It was the same vehicle used at the weddings of William and Kate and Prince Charles and Camilla.

After months of speculation, Meghan finally revealed her wedding dress, created by Clare Waight Keller, the British artistic director of the French fashion house Givenchy. The beautiful bride stepped out of the Rolls-Royce into glorious sunshine to reveal a stunning pure white gown, with an open bateau boat neckline.

The lines of the gown extended towards the back where the train flowed in soft round folds cushioned by an underskirt in triple silk organza. Keller also designed a veil representing the distinctive flora of each Commonwealth country united in one spectacular floral composition. The five-metre-long veil was made from silk tulle, with a trim of hand-embroidered flowers in silk

*Previous pages: Meghan
arrives at St George's Chapel*

*Left: Prince Harry and his
brother make their way to
the chapel*

threads and organza. Perhaps the most striking feature
was a diamond bandeau tiara, loaned to Meghan by the
Queen. The stunning tiara was made for Queen Mary in
1932, and hasn't been seen at a formal occasion since it
was worn by Princess Margaret in 1965.

A LOVING BOUQUET

In a simple, loving touch, Prince Harry handpicked several
flowers from the couple's private garden at Kensington
Palace to add to the bespoke bridal bouquet designed
by florist Philippa Craddock.

The spring blooms included forget-me-nots, which
were the favourite flower of Diana, Princess of Wales.
The couple specifically chose them to be included in the
bride's bouquet to honour the memory of Harry's late mother

Meghan's bouquet was a petite design, pulled together
in a gentle, ethereal, relaxed style with delicate blooms
also including scented sweet pea, lily of the valley, astilbe,
jasmine and astrantia and sprigs of myrtle, all bound with
a naturally dyed, raw silk ribbon.

The myrtle sprigs come from stems planted at Osborne
House on the Isle of Wight by Queen Victoria in 1845, and
from a plant grown from the myrtle used in the Queen's
wedding bouquet of 1947.

The 10 young bridesmaids and page boys – including
Prince George and Princess Charlotte – rose to the occasion.

"

The bride stepped out of the Rolls-Royce into glorious sunshine to reveal a stunning pure white gown, created by Clare Waight Keller, with an open bateau boat neckline

"

However, the excitement became too much for one of the younger ones who started crying just before Meghan entered the chapel.

With Meghan's father unable to attend it fell to the Prince of Wales to walk his soon-to-be daughter-in-law down the aisle. Prince Harry – like his best man, his older brother the Duke of Cambridge – was immaculate in the blue doeskin frockcoat uniform of the Blues and Royals, and both bearing the rank of Major. As Prince Charles handed the stunning bride to him, Harry touchingly , "Thanks Pa." At the altar, Harry, emotional and bursting with love and pride, told his stunning bride: "You look amazing."

A TRANSATLANTIC TWIST

The service combined tradition with a fresh modernity as well as the bride's African-American heritage. One of the highlights was Karen Gibson and The Kingdom Choir's performance of Leiber and Stoller's soul classic "Stand By Me", a song made famous by Ben E King.

The Most Reverend Bishop Michael Curry, the presiding bishop and primate of the American Episcopal Church, gave a lengthy and moving address. "There's power, power in love," said Bishop Curry, who was invited to speak by Meghan. "If you don't believe me, think about a time when you first fell in love. The whole world seemed to centre around you and your beloved." He concluded the passionate address saying he had better wrap up as "we gotta get y'all married!"

The couple then exchanged vows and rings, carried to the chapel by the Duke of Cambridge. In her vows, Ms

*Previous pages: The stunning bride
makes her way down the aisle*

*Opposite: The royal couple
exchange their vows*

Markle did not promise to "obey" her husband, while the prince broke with royal tradition by choosing to wear a wedding ring. The bride's ring (made by the London-based jewellers Cleave and Company) was fashioned from a piece of Welsh gold, gifted by to her by Her Majesty The Queen. Harry's ring was a platinum band with a textured finish.

When the Archbishop of Canterbury declared that they were husband and wife, a huge cheer run around the Berkshire town, where a throng of an estimated 100,000 people stood beyond the castle walls watching the ceremony on specially erected big screens amid a carnival atmosphere.

Inside the Gothic chapel, with its magnificent fan-vaulted ceiling that dates back to the reign of Henry VII, the guests – including Prince Harry's grandmother Her Majesty The Queen and his father the Prince of Wales –beamed with joy as the happy event unfolded.

The Prince of Wales graciously took Meghan's mother Doria Ragland's hand as they left to sign the register for the Royal Wedding of his son and Doria's daughter. As the register was being signed, 19-year-old cellist Sheku Kanneh-Mason – winner of the 2016 BBC's Young Musician of the Year competition – performed pieces by Fauré, Schubert and Maria Theresia von Paradis. He was accompanied by musicians from the BBC National Orchestra of Wales, the English Chamber Orchestra and the Philharmonia.

After an extract from a symphony by William Boyce (a former Master of the King's Music) and a performance of "God Save The Queen", Karen Gibson's London-based gospel choir also performed a version of Etta James's uplifting "Amen (This Little Light of Mine)" as the newlyweds left the chapel

After the service, the couple – who will now be known as the Duke and Duchess of Sussex after the Queen conferred the title on them – kissed in front of cheering well-wishers on the steps of the chapel.

A confident, beaming Meghan made the first move.

"Do we kiss now?" she said.

"Yes," her husband replied.

The couple then set off through Windsor in a horse-drawn open-carriage along a route lined by tens of thousands of well-wishers. Mingling among them in the bright sunshine were media crews from around the world, with TV cameras that overlooked Windsor High Street from every possible vantage point to capture the couple as they emerged through the castle gates.

Later, Prince Harry, 33, dressed in black tie, drove his wife – now changed into a lily-white, silk crepe Stella McCartney halter-neck dress – to Frogmore House for the second reception in a silver blue E-type Jaguar, with a registration plate that referenced the date – E190518. Manufactured in 1968, the car has since been converted to electric power. In a nod to Harry's late mother, Diana, Princess of Wales, he had given Meghan an aquamarine ring from her collection.

Meghan's absent father Thomas, 73, the subject of so much negative publicity in the tabloids in the lead-up to the wedding, reportedly watched the ceremony from California as he recovered from surgery. He told the US celebrity website, TMZ – which had become his chosen mouthpiece following his reported collusion with the paparazzi over staged photos of him that had threatened to derail proceedings – "My baby looks beautiful and she looks very happy."

Doria Ragland, who had stayed with her daughter overnight before accompanying her to the chapel, was dressed in a pale green Oscar de la Renta dress, with a neat hat. An emotional-looking Ms Ragland sat alone on the bride's side of the chapel for some time.

The wedding was one of the major global news events of the year; the hottest ticket in town. But, unlike his brother Prince William's wedding to Catherine Middleton (later the Duke and Duchess of Cambridge), which took place at Westminster Abbey on 29 April 2011 with 1,900 guests present, it was always going to be, at least relatively, a much smaller, more intimate affair.

A REGAL SETTING

Harry and Meghan's venue, St George's Chapel – a Church of England parish within Windsor Castle – has a capacity of only 800 people. From flowers to seating plans, the happy couple took charge of their

"
Guests included Oprah Winfrey, George and Amal Clooney, David and Victoria Beckham, Idris Elba, James Corden, Tom Hardy, Serena Williams and Sir Elton John, who later performed at the reception
"

Opposite, top: The Most Reverend Bishop Michael Curry gives his moving address

Opposite, bottom: The Royal Family look on

ceremony, which was designed to embrace those close to them, and also to welcome the public in to enjoy this life-changing moment.

Each of the 600 lucky guests invited to the actual wedding – including the Royal Family, members of Meghan's family and the couple's friends – received a stiff white card sent out in late March, with a select 200 close friends invited to a "VVIP" after-party at Frogmore House, the 17th-century estate just south of Windsor Castle where Harry and Meghan spent time together as their relationship blossomed. The formal burnished gold-and-black invitations with gilded edging, produced by Barnard and Westwood (holder of the Royal Warrant for Printing & Bookbinding by Appointment to Her Majesty The Queen since 1985, as well as one with her heir) were sent from the Prince of Wales for the 19 May noon service at St George's Chapel, Windsor.

However, Harry and Meghan made it clear that they wanted to share the wedding with as many members of the public as they could. They thus invited a further 2,640 lucky members of the general public to Windsor Castle to watch the bride, groom and wedding guests arrive.

Buckingham Palace confirmed that 1,200 members of the public "from every corner of the United Kingdom" were allowed into the castle grounds, chosen by nine regional Lord Lieutenant offices. The couple wanted these guests to come from a broad range of backgrounds and ages, including young people who have shown strong leadership, and those who have served their communities. It was a nice gesture. A further 200 people from Prince Harry's charities, as well as 100 school pupils, 610 Windsor Castle community members, and 530 members of the Royal Households and Crown Estate also received the coveted invites.

The couple also wanted to embrace the wider public. Knowing that thousands of people would travel to Windsor to soak up the atmosphere, they included a ride in an open landau carriage through the streets of Windsor in their plans. This tour, their first public appearance as man and wife, saw them being greeted by cheering well-wishers as the carriage made its way via Castle Hill, along the High Street and through Windsor Town before returning along the Long Walk for their receptions.

It would not have been a Royal Wedding without the involvement of military personnel and the splendour they bring to an occasion. The Queen is Commander-in-Chief of the British Armed Forces and, as sovereign and head of state, is also the Head of the Armed Forces. All military personnel vow "to serve Queen and country".

CEREMONIAL SUPPORT

Regiments and units that hold a special relationship with Prince Harry provided ceremonial support at the wedding and during the carriage procession at the request of Kensington Palace, with more than 250 members of the Armed Forces performing ceremonial duties. Members of the Household Cavalry formed a staircase party at St George's Chapel, while the State Trumpeters and a Captain's Escort from the Household Cavalry provided ceremonial support.

Captain Harry Wales – as he was known in the army – joined the Blues and Royals in April 2006 and served with the Household Cavalry Regiment, undertaking two tours of Afghanistan and rising to the rank of Captain. Royal Marines were also on duty as Harry is Captain General Royal Marines, the ceremonial head of the force, after succeeding the Duke of Edinburgh in the role in December 2017.

There were personnel from 3 Regiment Army Air Corps on duty too, as Harry served as an Apache pilot in Helmand Province, Afghanistan with 662 Squadron, 3 Regiment Army Air Corps. The Royal Gurkha Rifles were also present, as

Harry served with the 1st Battalion The Royal Gurkha Rifles in Afghanistan in 2007. They were joined by personnel from RAF Honington, as Harry is Honorary Air Commandant of RAF Honington. Musical support to the street liners was provided by the Band of the Irish Guards.

Streets within the precincts of Windsor Castle were lined by members of the Windsor Castle Guard from 1st Battalion the Irish Guards and by Armed Forces personnel from the Royal Navy Small Ships and Diving, as Harry is Commodore-in-Chief, Small Ships and Diving.

"I am proud that members of the Armed Forces have been asked to take part in the ceremonial celebrations taking place on the royal couple's wedding day," said Air Chief Marshal Sir Stuart Peach, Chief of the Defence Staff. "It is a happy occasion for the whole country and reminds us of the role the Armed Forces play in marking important events in the life of the nation. I am particularly pleased to hear that members of the Armed Forces who have a close relationship with Prince Harry will be taking part. Servicemen and women from the Royal Navy, Army and Royal Air Force will all be honoured to offer their support."

Harry and Meghan were delighted that members of the Armed Forces could play such a special role in their wedding. "The military, and these units in particular, hold a great significance for Prince Harry and the couple are incredibly grateful for their support," said a Kensington Palace spokesperson.

A FAMILY AFFAIR

The core aspects of the wedding – including the church service, associated music, flowers, decorations and reception – were paid for by the groom's father, the Prince of Wales. The Duke of Cambridge, Prince William, was always expected to be Harry's best man, or "supporter". When an interviewer asked about the possibility of him being best man, William responded: "He hasn't asked me yet." He then added, with a laugh, "So, it could be a sensitive issue."

Harry's nephew and niece Prince George and Princess Charlotte were among the page boys and flower girls. The ceremony was conducted by the Dean of Windsor, the Right Revd. David Conner. Officiating as the couple took their marriage vows was the Archbishop of Canterbury, Justin Welby. He also baptised Meghan into the Church of England a few months before the wedding day, describing it as "beautiful, sincere and very moving". Archbishop Welby jokingly disclosed that his biggest concerns ahead of the Royal Wedding was dropping the rings and forgetting the vows.

The Archbishop formed a close bond with the engaged couple as they readied themselves for the big day. In an interview before the ceremony, he said: "You know, at the heart of it are two people who have fallen in love with each other, who are committing their lives to each other with the most beautiful words and profound thoughts, who do it in the presence of God." He added: "You just focus on the couple. It's their day."

A DAZZLING GUEST LIST

Guests at the wedding included Oprah Winfrey, George and Amal Clooney, David and Victoria Beckham, Idris Elba and his fiancé Sabrina Dhowre, James Corden and his wife Julia Carey, actor Tom Hardy, Argentine polo player Nacho

*Opposite: The royal couple
exchange a kiss as they leave
the chapel*

Figueras, and Indian actress Priyanka Chopra. Sir Elton John. who later performed at the first wedding reception, was there with his husband David Furnish. Serena Williams, a close friend of Meghan's, was also at the ceremony, joined by her husband Alexis Ohanian, the co-founder of Reddit.

They joined Her Majesty the Queen and more than 30 members of the Royal Family to witness the ceremony, alongside the bride and groom's trusted inner circle of friends. Prince Harry's much-loved former nannies Tiggy Legge-Bourke, now Tiggy Pettifer, and Jessie Webb were also invited to witness their young charge's milestone day. Even Harry's ex-girlfriends Chelsy Davy and Cressida Bonas took their places in the chapel.

Among the royals were the Duke of York, his former wife Sarah Ferguson, Duchess of York and their daughters (and Harry's cousins) Princesses Beatrice and Eugenie. The Earl of Wessex (the Queen's youngest son Edward) and the Countess of Wessex (Edward's wife since 1999) were there, as was Lady Louise Mountbatten-Windsor – the Duke of Cambridge's 14-year-old cousin, daughter of the Earl and Countess of Wessex. Also present was James, Viscount Severn, Edward and Sophie's 10-year-old son and the 11th in line to the throne.

The Princess Royal – the Queen and the Duke of Edinburgh's only daughter – was present with Vice Admiral Sir Tim Laurence, the Queen's son-in-law, who has been married to Princess Anne since 1992. Mr Peter Phillips – the Queen's eldest grandson, who was married in Windsor Castle in 2008, was present with his Canadian bride Autumn Kelly. They have two children.

Jack Brooksbank – the fiancé of Princess Eugenie, due to marry later in 2018, was also there. Mrs Emilie van Cutsem, the widow of Prince Charles's late close friend Hugh van Cutsem, was also invited, as was Mrs Amanda Ward, the widow of Harry's godfather Gerald Ward.

One of the loudest cheers was reserved for the Duke of Edinburgh – Prince Philip, 96 – who has just recovered from hip surgery. Walking in and out of the chapel, he seemed as sprightly and as upright as ever.

MEETING THE PUBLIC

It was a day of love and celebration as thousands of well-wishers poured into Windsor in the hope of seeing the couple in the only true public part of the wedding – the carriage ride. The newlyweds did not disappoint, delighting the huge crowds, many waving union flags, and sharing a second kiss on the carriage ride through Windsor following their nuptials.

They were enthusiastically cheered on during the royal procession by delighted crowds as they were whisked away for the procession. Harry and Meghan held hands and beamed at each other as the carriage pulled up to the chapel. Excitement spilled over as the bride and groom shared a second tender kiss after having their first on the steps of St George's Chapel.

Meghan had waved at the jubilant crowd as she and Harry set off for the 30-minute journey through Windsor.

Opposite: *The Duchess of Cambridge and Princess Charlotte on the steps of St George's*

The couple couldn't stop smiling as they left the modern ceremony to the delight of cheering crowds who have been waiting in Windsor all week for a glimpse of the royal kiss.

The streets were lined with union jack bunting as the couple were pulled by horses in an open-topped Ascot Landau carriage. There are five Ascot Landaus kept by the Royal Mews – with one featured in the carriage procession following the wedding of Kate Middleton and Prince William in 2011. Well-wishers waved banners as they caught a glimpse of the couple – with some queuing overnight for a chance to see the newlyweds on their big day.

Following the carriage ride around Windsor and all the public adulation, the happy couple rode back into Windsor Castle and stepped into St George's Hall – the venue for royal weddings for centuries, notably that of the Prince of Wales and the Duchess of Cornwall in 2005 – for the first of two receptions.

For their wedding cake, Harry and Meghan chose the pastry chef Claire Ptak, owner of the Violet Bakery in Hackney, east London, to create a lemon elderflower cake to incorporate the bright flavours of spring. Covered with buttercream and decorated with fresh flowers it was a work of art.

"I can't tell you how delighted I am to be chosen to make Prince Harry and Ms Markle's wedding cake," said Claire. "Knowing that they really share the same values as I do about food provenance, sustainability, seasonality and – most importantly – flavour, makes this the most exciting event to be a part of." Meghan had previously interviewed the California-raised Ptak for her former lifestyle website TheTig.com, where she celebrated food and travel, and featured interviews with friends and role models to discuss philanthropy and community.

A GLOBAL CELEBRATION

As the role of the British Royal Family has evolved to be more symbolic, so royal weddings have followed suit. In the past, prior to the late 19th century, such unions were relatively low-key affairs that consummated alliances between countries and kingdoms. This begun to change under Queen Victoria's reign, when the royal weddings of her children and grandchildren started to become extravagant affairs attracting big crowds that filled the streets. But it was not until the age of television that the vast pulling power of royal weddings emerged.

Opposite: Family members and friends savour the occasion in the May sunshine

In 1981, the wedding of Harry's father and mother, Prince Charles and Lady Diana Spencer, was watched by a global audience of 750 million people, a sixth of the world's population. The global audience exceeded well over a billion souls when Harry's brother Prince William married Catherine in 2011. Harry and Meghan's wedding attracted huge viewing figures, especially with Meghan being an American. As the great Victorian essayist, journalist and constitutional expert Walter Bagehot wrote years ago, "a princely marriage is the brilliant edition of a universal fact, and, as such, it rivets mankind".

Bagehot is right. This amazing spectacle was not only Harry and Meghan's wedding, it was embraced by all those who watched. And those who celebrated – either by attending, by cheering on the streets of Windsor or by watching on television – were delighted to be a part of it too.

In a sense it was a traditional wedding – the dress, the bridesmaids, the vows, the hymns. But it was in its own charming way unconventional and felt fresh.

A VERY MODERN RECEPTION

Harry and Meghan, now Their Royal Highnesses The Duke and Duchess of Sussex, always said they wanted the wedding to reflect them and their love for each other, and it certainly did that.

The result was a modern, inclusive, uplifting wedding for a modern, diverse couple. This wedding was about the future, as the modern Royal Family spreads its wings.

At the first reception Sir Elton John – a close friend of Diana, Princess of Wales, who sung so movingly at Diana's funeral – performed three songs for the couple. As well as singing "I'm Still Standing" and "Circle Of Life", he dedicated his 1972 hit "Tiny Dancer" to the beautiful bride.

Prince Charles, a drily comic speaker, had the guests in stitches with stories of his little boy and in tears when he spoke with pride of the man Harry had become. Harry too was on good form at the reception. The new Duke of Sussex also had a few jokes up his sleeve, as might be expected of the Royal Family's resident jester. "Don't pinch the swords," he told an audience, who were surrounded by more suits of armour than Agincourt. It was nice of everyone to make such an effort, he added, especially since he and his bride had only wanted "a low-key wedding".

Inside the second "very private" wedding reception at Frogmore House, guests were treated to dirty burgers, candyfloss and cocktails, including one titled "When Harry

"

At the heart of it are two people who have fallen in love with each other, who are committing their lives to each other with the most beautiful words and profound thoughts

"

*Right: Crowds line
the Long Walk*

*Overleaf: The newly
married Duke and
Duchess of Sussex
leave Windsor Castle
to attend their
evening reception*

Met Meghan", featuring rum and ginger (a nod to Harry's
red hair). There was also a "naughty" best man speech from
Prince William, as well as numerous other hijinks. And, with
another break with royal tradition, the bride, an independent
woman, spoke too of her profound love for her husband.

DJ Sam Totolee, who played the club track "I Took a Pill in
Ibiza" at Pippa Middleton's wedding to James Matthews, got
the 200 glamorous guests busting out moves on the dance
floor. Actor Idris Elba even tried his hand at spinning records
during the evening.

The music on offer had a distinctly R&B-tinged flavour,
working from 1960s soul classics through to dance hits of
the '80s and '90s. There was no orthodox "first-dance" tune
for the couple. Instead, the DJ played the Whitney Houston
hit "I Wanna Dance With Somebody", and all 200 guests
took to the dance floor.

And it all ended in spectacular fashion with an explosion
of fireworks that lit up the Windsor night sky.

THE MARRIAGE OF
HIS ROYAL HIGHNESS PRINCE HENRY OF WALES
WITH MS MEGHAN MARKLE

ORDER OF SERVICE

———

*The following Pastoral Introduction
is taken from Common Worship*

A WEDDING is one of life's great moments, a time of solemn commitment as well as good wishes, feasting and joy. St John tells us how Jesus shared in such an occasion at Cana, and gave there a sign of new beginnings as he turned water into wine.

Marriage is intended by God to be a creative relationship, as his blessing enables husband and wife to love and support each other in good times and in bad, and to share in the care and upbringing of children. For Christians, marriage is also an invitation to share life together in the spirit of Jesus Christ. It is based upon a solemn, public and life-long covenant between a man and a woman, declared and celebrated in the presence of God and before witnesses.

On this their wedding day the bride and bridegroom face each other, make their promises and receive God's blessing. You are witnesses of the marriage, and express your support by your presence and your prayers. Your support does not end today: the couple will value continued encouragement in the days and years ahead of them.

St. George's Chapel

Set in the lower ward of Windsor Castle, St George's Chapel is a building of rare beauty, begun in 1475 by King Edward IV. The Chapel, built in the striking English Perpendicular Gothic style of the period, was intended both to be a new and fitting home for the College of St George and the Order of the Garter (founded over a century previously in 1348), and to be a Royal Chapel in which the Sovereign and the Royal Family might worship God and to which they might come on various occasions—some solemn, and many, like today's wedding or the Garter Service next month, celebratory—to receive God's blessing and to hear prayer offered in God's presence. The Opus Dei, or daily round of prayer, is offered by the members of the College who live in the precincts of the Chapel and whose duty it is to pray morning and evening for the Sovereign and the Companions of the Order of the Garter. There are twenty- three services each week, all of which are open to members of the public.

Perhaps the Chapel's most striking feature is the vaulted stone roof of very wide span, held up only by the light and graceful walls and the external flying buttresses. Most of the coloured bosses on the roof of the Chapel bear the badges and arms of King Henry VII and those of his servants who helped to build part of the Chapel, finished in 1528. The boss in the roof over the Organ Screen bears the arms of King Henry VIII, who is buried in a vault beneath the Quire of the Chapel. The great coloured glass West Window is one of the finest in England and is said to be the third largest in the country; in seventy-five lights, the vast majority of which date from between 1503 and 1509, it depicts a host of warrior saints, archbishops and kings and, in the bottom right hand corner, with hammer in hand the likeness of William Vertue the mason and architect responsible for the building of the Nave and Quire Vault.

Those seated in the Quire of the Chapel are able to see one of the Chapel's greatest treasures, the carved oak stalls dating from between 1478 and 1485. Each stall is a work of art and a triumph of craftsmanship, each unique in its detail. Above each of the Companions' stalls hangs his or her banner and on the canopy of a Knight's stall is his helmet and crest and sword of knighthood, symbolically half-drawn from its scabbard to show his readiness to take up arms in defence of the Sovereign and the realm. The Lady Companions do not bear arms. On the back of the stalls are nearly 800 plates which commemorate Knights of the Garter past and present.

On the High Altar is a jewelled Cross, given by Queen Victoria, and two silver- gilt candlesticks dating from the reign of King Charles II. Also displayed are three gilt dishes of very great size, elaborately embossed; one was intended to have been the gift of Mary of Orange, sister of King Charles II, while the other two smaller dishes are the gift of Anne Hyde, Duchess of York, wife of the future King James II.

Looking down on the Quire from above is the wooden oriel window installed in the Chantry Chapel of King Edward IV by King Henry VIII so that his Queen, Katherine of Aragon, might watch the ceremonies of the Installation of Knights of the Garter in the Quire below. The window bears the arms of Henry and Katherine and the intertwined Tudor Rose of England and the Pomegranate of Aragon. It has frequently been used as a Royal Pew or watching chamber and it was from this vantage point that Queen Victoria watched the wedding in the Chapel below of her son, the Prince of Wales, to Princess Alexandra of Denmark on 10 March 1863. It was at this same wedding that the fine East Window, created by Messrs Clayton and Bell in commemoration of the late Prince Albert, was first seen.

Prayer

GOD of love,
send your blessing upon Harry and Meghan,
and all who are joined in marriage,
that, rejoicing in your will
and continuing under your protection,
they may both live and grow
in your love all their days,
through Jesus Christ our Lord.
Amen

© The Church of England

The Service

*The service is led by The Right Reverend
David Conner KCVO, Dean of Windsor.*

*The marriage is solemnized by The Most Reverend and
Right Honourable Justin Welby, Archbishop of Canterbury.*

*The service is sung by the choir of St George's Chapel,
conducted by Mr James Vivian,*

*Director of Music, St George's Chapel. The Organ is played
by Mr Luke Bond, Assistant*

*Director of Music, St George's Chapel, Windsor, and Mr Jason Richards,
Organ Scholar, St George's Chapel.*

*The 'Cellist, Mr Sheku Kanneh-Mason is a British 'Cellist who
won the 2016 BBC Young Musician of the Year award.*

*The Orchestra is made up of musicians drawn from the BBC National
Orchestra of Wales, the English Chamber Orchestra and the Philharmonia,
conducted by Mr Christopher Warren-Green.*

*For the Procession of the Bride, they are joined by:
Ms Elin Manahan Thomas (Soprano) and Mr David Blackadder (Trumpet).*

Ms Karen Gibson and The Kingdom Choir.

The State Trumpeters of the Household Cavalry.

Music before the service

From 10.35 am Mr Luke Bond, Assistant Director of Music, will play

Marche Hèroïque | Sir Alfred Herbert Brewer (1865–1928)

Prelude and Fugue in G Major, BWV 541 | Johann Sebastian Bach (1685–1750)

Psalm-Prelude Set 1, No. 2 | Herbert Howells (1892–1983)

Symphony No. 4, Andante Cantabile | Charles-Marie Widor (1844–1937)

Prelude on 'Rhosymedre' | Ralph Vaughan Williams (1872–1958)

From 11.10 am the Orchestra will play

Salut d'Amour | Sir Edward Elgar (1857–1934)

St Paul's Suite, movement 4 | Gustav Holst (1874–1934)

Lady Radnor's Suite, movements 2, 3 & | Sir Charles Hubert Hastings Parry (1848–1914)

Capriol Suite, movements 2, 3, & 5 | Peter Warlock (1894–1930)

Fantasia on Greensleeves | Ralph Vaughan Williams

Serenade for Strings, movement 1 | Sir Edward Elgar

Chanson de Matin | Sir Edward Elgar arr. Benjamin Woodgates (b. 1986)

At 11.25 am Members of the Royal Family arrive at the Galilee Porch and are received by the Dean of Windsor who presents the Canons of Windsor and the Archbishop of Canterbury. Those in the Quire stand as they are conducted to their places.

All sit.

At 11.40 am The Bridegroom and his Best Man arrive at the West Door and are received by the Dean of Windsor. All stand as the Bridegroom and his Best Man are conducted to the Bray Chantry Chapel.

At 11.42 am Their Royal Highnesses The Prince of Wales and The Duchess of Cornwall arrive at the Galilee Porch and are received by the Vice-Dean who presents the Canons of Windsor and the Archbishop of Canterbury. Those in the Quire stand as they are conducted to their places.

At 11.45 am the Mother of the Bride, Ms Doria Ragland, arrives at the Galilee Porch and is received by the Dean of Windsor and is conducted to her seat in the Quire.

At 11.52 am Her Majesty The Queen arrives at the Galilee Porch and is received by the Dean of Windsor who presents the Canons of Windsor and the Archbishop of Canterbury. Those in the Quire stand as Her Majesty is conducted to her place in the Quire.

A fanfare will sound.

All stand as the Choir and Clergy move in procession to the Quire.

Sactristan

The Choir of St George's Chapel, Windsor Castle

The Director of Music – Mr James Vivian

Minor Canon - The Reverend Franklin Lee

Chaplain to The Queen – The Reverend Prebendary Rose Hudson-Wilkin

Coptic Orthodox Archbishop of London – His Eminence Archbishop Angaelos

Presiding Bishop and Primate of the Episcopal Church in the USA -The Most Reverend Michael Curry

The Archbishop of Canterbury – The Most Reverend and Right Honourable Justin Welby

Canon Steward – The Reverend Canon Dr Mark Powell

Canon Precentor – The Reverend Canon Martin Poll

Vice-Dean – The Reverend Canon Dr Hueston Finlay

All sit
At the entrance of the Bride, all stand.
A fanfare will sound at the Bride's arrival.

The Bride, having been greeted by the Dean of Windsor, moves in procession
through the Nave where she is joined by her Father, Mr Thomas Markle,
to the High Altar. The Bridegroom and his Best Man await.

Introit

Performed by the Orchestra and Ms Elin Manahan Thomas (Soprano) with
Mr David Blackadder (Trumpet).

ETERNAL source of light divine,
With double warmth thy beams display,
And with distinguished glory shine,
To add a lustre to this day.
George Frederick Handel (1685–1759)

All remain standing.
At the High Altar, The Dean of Windsor greets the congregation.

THE Grace of our Lord Jesus Christ,
the love of God,
and the fellowship of the Holy Spirit be with you:
and also with you.
God is love, and those who live in love live in God and God lives in them.
1 John 4. 16

The Preface

All sit. The Dean of Windsor reads

IN the presence of God, Father, Son and Holy Spirit, we have come together to witness the marriage of HENRY CHARLES ALBERT DAVID and RACHEL MEGHAN, to pray for God's blessing on them, to share their joy and to celebrate their love. Marriage is a gift of God in creation through which husband and wife may know the grace of God. It is given that as man and woman grow together in love and trust, they shall be united with one another in heart, body and mind, as Christ is united with his bride, the Church. The gift of marriage brings husband and wife together in the delight and tenderness of sexual union and joyful commitment to the end of their lives. It is given as the foundation of family life in which children are born and nurtured and in which each member of the family, in good times and in bad, may find strength, companionship and comfort, and grow to maturity in love. Marriage is a way of life made holy by God, and blessed by the presence of our Lord Jesus Christ with those celebrating a wedding at Cana in Galilee. Marriage is a sign of unity and loyalty which all should uphold and honour. It enriches society and strengthens community. No one should enter into it lightly or selfishly but reverently and responsibly in the sight of almighty God. HARRY and MEGHAN are now to enter this way of life. They will each give their consent to the other and make solemn vows, and in token of this they will each give and receive a ring. We pray with them that the Holy Spirit will guide and strengthen them, that they may fulfil God's purposes for the whole of their earthly life together.

All stand

The Hymn

LORD of all hopefulness, Lord of all joy,
Whose trust, ever child-like,
no cares could destroy,
Be there at our waking, and give us, we pray,
Your bliss in our hearts, Lord,
at the break of the day.

Lord of all eagerness, Lord of all faith,
Whose strong hands
were skilled at the plane and the lathe,
Be there at our labours, and give us, we pray,
Your strength in our hearts, Lord,
at the noon of the day.

Lord of all kindliness, Lord of all grace,
Your hands swift to welcome,
your arms to embrace,
Be there at our homing, and give us, we pray,
Your love in our hearts, Lord,
at the eve of the day.

Jan Struther (1901–53) 'Slane', Traditional Irish Melody

All remain standing as the Archbishop leads

The Declarations

FIRST, I am required to ask anyone present who knows a reason why these persons may
not lawfully marry, to declare it now.

The Archbishop says to the Couple

THE vows you are about to take are to be made in the presence of God,
who is judge of all and knows all the secrets of our hearts; therefore if either of you knows
a reason why you may not lawfully marry, you must declare it now.

The Archbishop says to the Bridegroom

HARRY, will you take MEGHAN to be your wife? Will you love her, comfort her, honour and protect
her, and, forsaking all others, be faithful to her as long as you both shall live?

He answers

I will.

The Archbishop says to the Bride

MEGHAN, will you take HARRY to be your husband? Will you love him, comfort him, honour and
protect him, and, forsaking all others, be faithful to him as long as you both shall live?

She answers

I will.

The Archbishop says to the congregation

WILL you, the families and friends of HARRY and MEGHAN, support and uphold them
in their marriage now and in the years to come?

All answer

We will.

The Archbishop invites the people to pray, silence is kept and he says

GOD our Father, from the beginning
you have blessed creation with abundant life.
Pour out your blessings upon HARRY and MEGHAN,
that they may be joined in mutual love and companionship,
in holiness and commitment to each other.

We ask this through our Lord Jesus Christ your Son,
who is alive and reigns with you,
in the unity of the Holy Spirit, one God, now and for ever. Amen.

All sit.

Reading

from the Song of Solomon
read by The Lady Jane Fellowes from the Nave

MY beloved speaks and says to me: 'Arise, my love, my fair one, and come away; for now the winter is past, the rain is over and gone. The flowers appear on the earth; the time of singing has come, and the voice of the turtle-dove is heard in our land.

The fig tree puts forth its figs, and the vines are in blossom; they give forth fragrance.

Arise, my love, my fair one, and come away.' Set me as a seal upon your heart, as a seal upon your arm; for love is strong as death, passion fierce as the grave. Its flashes are flashes of fire, a raging flame. Many waters cannot quench love, neither can floods drown it.

If one offered for love all the wealth of one's house, it would be utterly scorned.

All remain seated while the Choir of St George's Chapel sing

Motet

If ye love me

IF ye love me,
keep my commandments,
and I will pray the Father,
and he shall give you another comforter, that he may 'bide with you forever,
e'en the spirit of truth.
Thomas Tallis (1505–85)

All remain seated.

The Address

by The Most Reverend Michael Curry

All remain seated.

Karen Gibson and The Kingdom Choir will sing 'Stand by me'
from the West End of The Chapel.
WHEN the night has come,
And the land is dark,
And the moon is the only light we see. No, I won't be afraid.
Oh, I won't be afraid,
Just as long as you stand, stand by me. So darling, darling, stand by me,
Oh, stand by me.
Oh stand, stand by me. Stand by me.

If the sky that we look upon,
Should tumble and fall,
Or the mountain should crumble to the sea. I won't cry, I won't cry.
No, I won't shed a tear.
Just as long as you stand, stand by me, Darling, darling, stand by me...
Whenever you're in trouble,
Won't you stand by me, oh stand by me. Oh stand, stand by me. Stand by me.

Jerry Leiber (1933–2011) Ben E. King (1938–2015) and Mike Stroller (b. 1933)
arr by Mark Delisser (b. 1973)

All remain seated as the Archbishop leads

The Vows

HARRY and MEGHAN, I now invite you to join hands and make your vows, in the presence of God and his people.

The Bride and Bridegroom face each other and join hands. The Bridegroom says

I HARRY, take you, MEGHAN, to be my wife, to have and to hold from , this day forward; for better, for worse, for richer, for poorer, in sickness and in health, to love and to cherish, till death us do part; according to God's holy law. In the presence of God I make this vow.

The Bride says

I MEGHAN, take you, HARRY, to be my husband, to have and to hold , from this day forward; for better, for worse, for richer, for poorer, in sickness and in health, to love and to cherish, till death us do part; according to God's holy law. In the presence of God I make this vow.

They loose hands.

The giving of the rings

HEAVENLY Father, by your blessing let these rings be to HARRY and MEGHAN a symbol of unending love and faithfulness, to remind them of the vow and covenant which they have made this day, through Jesus Christ our Lord. Amen.

The Bridegroom places the ring on the fourth finger
of the Bride's left hand and, holding it there, says

MEGHAN, I give you this ring as a sign of our marriage. With my body I honour you, all that I am I give to you, and all that I have I share with you, within the love of God, Father, Son and Holy Spirit.

They loose hands and the Bride places a ring on the fourth finger
of the Bridegroom's left hand and, holding it there, says

HARRY, I give you this ring as a sign of our marriage. With my body I honour you, all that I am I give to you, and all that I have I share with you, within the love of God, Father, Son and Holy Spirit.

All remain seated.

The Proclamation

The Archbishop addresses the people

IN the presence of God, and before this congregation, HARRY and MEGHAN have given their consent and made their marriage vows to each other. They have declared their marriage by the joining of hands and by the giving and receiving of rings. I therefore proclaim that they are husband and wife

The Archbishop joins their right hands together and says
Those whom God has joined together let no one put asunder.

All remain seated while the Choir of St George's Chapel sing

THE ANTHEM
The Lord bless you and keep you
THE Lord bless you and keep you:
The Lord make his face to shine upon you,
to shine upon you and be gracious unto you.
The Lord lift up the light of his countenance upon you,
John Rutter (b. 1945)

All remain seated.

The blessing of the marriage

The Archbishop says

BLESSED are you, O Lord our God, for you have created joy and gladness, pleasure and delight, love, peace and fellowship. Pour out the abundance of your blessing upon HARRY and MEGHAN in their new life together. Let their love for each other be a seal upon their hearts and a crown upon their heads. Bless them in their work and in their companionship; awake and asleep, in joy and in sorrow, in life and in death. Finally, in your mercy, bring them to that banquet where your saints feast for ever in your heavenly home. We ask his through Jesus Christ your Son, our Lord, who lives and reigns with you and give you peace. Amen.

GOD the Father, God the Son, God the Holy Spirit, bless, preserve and keep you; the Lord mercifully grant you the riches of his grace, that you may please him both in body and soul, and, living together in faith and love, may receive the blessings of eternal life. Amen.

The Prayers

Led by Archbishop Angaelos and The Reverend Prebendary
Rose Hudson- Wilkin from the Nave.

FAITHFUL God, holy and eternal, source of life and spring of love, we thank and praise you for bringing HARRY and MEGHAN to this day, and we pray for them. Lord of life and love: hear our prayer.

MAY their marriage be life-giving and life-long, enriched by your presence and strengthened by your grace; may they bring comfort and confidence to each other in faithfulness and trust. Lord of life and love: hear our prayer.

MAY the hospitality of their home bring refreshment and joy to all around them; may their love overflow to neighbours in need and embrace those in distress Lord of life and love: hear our prayer.

MAY they discern in your word order and purpose for their lives; and may the power of your Holy Spirit lead them in truth and defend them in adversity. Lord of life and love: hear our prayer.

MAY they nurture their family with devotion, see their children grow in body, mind and spirit and come at last to the end of their lives with hearts content and in joyful anticipation of heaven. Lord of life and love: Hear our prayer.

Let us pray with confidence as our Saviour has taught us

OUR Father in heaven, hallowed be your name; your kingdom come, your will be done; on earth as in heaven. Give us today our daily bread. Forgive us our sins as we forgive those who sin against us. Lead us not into temptation but deliver us from evil. For the kingdom, the power, and the glory are yours, now and for ever. Amen.

All stand.

Hymn

GUIDE me, O thou great Redeemer,
Pilgrim through this barren land;
I am weak, but thou art mighty,
Hold me with thy powerful hand:
Bread of heaven,
Feed me till I want no more.

Open now the crystal fountain
Whence the healing stream doth flow;
Let the fire and cloudy pillar
Lead me all my journey through:
Strong deliverer,
Be thou still my strength and shield.

When I tread the verge of Jordan,
Bid my anxious fears subside;
Death of death, and hell's Destruction
Land me safe on Canaan's side:
Songs of praises
I will ever give to thee.

William Williams (1717–91)
'Cwm Rhondda', John Hughes (1873–1932)
Descant verse: James Vivian (b. 1974)

The Blessing

All remain standing as the Dean of Windsor says

GOD the Holy Trinity make you strong in faith and love, defend you on every side, and guide you in truth and peace; and the blessing of God almighty, the Father, the Son, and the Holy Spirit, be among you and remain with you always. Amen.

All remain standing.
The organ plays as those who are signing the registers
move from the Quire to the North Quire Aisle.
All sit at the conclusion of the organ music.
During the Signing of the Register the following is played
by Mr Sheku Kanneh-Mason and the Orchestra:

Sicilienne – Maria Theresia von Paradis (1759–1824) arr. Chris Hazell (b. 1948)
Après un rêve – Gabriel Fauré (1845–1924) arr. Chris Hazell
Ave Maria – Franz Schubert (1797–1828) arr. Chris Hazell

All stand as the Bride and Bridegroom return to the Quire

NATIONAL ANTHEM
GOD save our gracious Queen,
Long live our noble Queen,
God save The Queen!
Send her victorious,
Happy and glorious,
Long to reign over us, God save The Queen!

The procession of the Bride and Bridegroom

During the Procession the following is played
Symphony no. 1 in B-flat – Allegro, William Boyce (1711–1779)
Amen/This little light of mine – Etta James Jester Hairston (1901–2000)

All remain standing during the Procession of the Bride and Bridegroom,
until members of their families have left the Chapel.
All remain standing as the Ecclesiastical Procession leaves by
way of the Organ Screen and the North Quire Aisle.
Thereafter please leave the Chapel as directed by the Lay Stewards.
Those in the Quire should leave by way of the South Door in order to stand
on Chapter Grass to view the Carriage procession on Chapel Hill.

Copyright © The Archbishops Council 2000, 2005
and Harry Dixon Loes (1892–1965)

Chapter Two

THE ENGAGEMENT

Following the official announcement
of Harry and Meghan's engagement in
November 2017, a picture soon emerged
of a happy and down-to-earth young
couple, who are clearly besotted
with each other

The announcement came in that most modern of ways – through an official statement from the Prince of Wales's office, Clarence House, issued via Twitter. The loving couple, Harry and Meghan, may only have been dating since the summer of 2016 but it came as no surprise, with media commentators predicting that this 16-month romance would result in marriage.

The official statement, issued on 27 November 2017, read: "His Royal Highness The Prince of Wales is delighted to announce the engagement of Prince Harry to Ms Meghan Markle. The wedding will take place in spring 2018. Further details about the wedding day will be announced in due course. His Royal Highness and Ms Markle became engaged in London earlier this month. Prince Harry has informed Her Majesty The Queen and other close members of his family. Prince Harry has also sought and received the blessing of Ms Markle's parents. The couple will live in Nottingham Cottage at Kensington Palace."

This was quickly followed by statements from the Queen and Prince Harry's brother Prince William. The Queen and the Duke of Edinburgh said they were "delighted" for their grandson and his bride-to-be, and "wish them every happiness". "We are very excited for Harry and Meghan," said the Duke and Duchess of Cambridge. "It has been wonderful getting to know Meghan and to see how happy she and Harry are together." Ms Markle's parents wished their daughter and Harry "a lifetime of happiness", adding that they were "incredibly happy" for Meghan and Harry.

*Previous pages and left:
Harry and Meghan make
their first public appearance
following the announcement
of their engagement in
the Sunken Garden at
Kensington Palace*

"Our daughter has always been a kind and loving person. To see her union with Harry, who shares the same qualities, is a source of great joy for us as parents." Visiting Poundbury in Dorset, the Prince of Wales said he was "thrilled" and "very happy indeed" for Prince Harry and Meghan.

A FIRST APPEARANCE

A few hours after the official announcement, the beaming couple made a public appearance together, carefully choreographed by the army of Buckingham Palace press officers, in the Sunken Garden at Kensington Palace. The location was chosen by Harry in a sentimental nod to his late mother, Princess Diana, who would often visit the garden seeking moments of contemplation as she admired the floral displays as they changed through spring and summer during her all too short lifetime.

Meghan, hand in hand with her prince, looked stunning in a white coat, produced by the Canadian brand Line the Label, and her dress by Italian designer Paolo Rossello's label P.A.R.O.S.H. The "Meghan effect" was already underway, it would appear, with Line the Label's website crashing shortly afterwards due to the number of people trying to access it. Her shoes, strappy Aquazzura Matilde Crisscross Nude Suede Pumps, proved just as popular. The royal bride-to-be then proudly showed off her three-stone diamond engagement ring, designed by Harry himself. It included two diamonds from the personal collection of Princess Diana, as well as a diamond from Botswana, where the couple vacationed to celebrate Meghan's 36th birthday. The band was made of gold and the ring was made by Cleave and Company, court jewellers and medallists to the Queen.

The couple braved the biting November cold to answer a number of questions from the waiting press, who were strategically separated from them by several metres of water. Harry and Meghan stood on

"
As a matter of fact,
I could barely let you
finish proposing, I said,
'Can I say yes now?'

"

the other side of the large ornamental pond before waving at the cameras and walking back through the garden, arm in arm.

Meghan is the first American to marry into the British Royal Family since Wallis Simpson, a twice divorced American socialite from Baltimore whose marriage to Edward VIII led to his abdication. However, it was a very different world back then, when divorce was regarded as unacceptable in society.

Meghan said that she was "so very happy, thank you" to be engaged to Harry. The Prince said he was "thrilled, over the moon" adding: "Very glad it's not raining, as well." They smiled and giggled throughout their appearance. When Harry was asked how he proposed, Ms Markle replied "Save that", with Harry adding: "That will come later." Answering questions posed by waiting journalists, the Prince laughed as he declared he knew his girlfriend was the one "the very first time we met", before they left with their arms around each other and heads affectionately close together.

THE INTERVIEW
In a 20-minute interview following their engagement announcement, the Prince and Meghan shared intimate details of their hopes – from having a family to setting off around the Commonwealth to carve out their joint future as working royals. Still giggling, they sat down in Kensington Palace for an interview with the BBC's Mishal Husain, revealing how they fell in love and conducted their long-distance love affair across the Atlantic.

"The fact that I fell in love with Meghan so incredible quickly was confirmation to me that all the stars have aligned and everything was just perfect," said a gushing Harry. It started, he said, with a blind date and they eventually fell in love under the stars in Botswana. He joked that when, on a meeting with

the Queen, her notoriously snappy corgis gave Meghan their seal of approval, he knew a royal wedding was inevitable.

Meghan revealed that Harry had proposed over a chicken dinner conducted in their "cosy" cottage. The couple, who saw each other every two weeks during the early stages of their relationship, disclosed how the Royal Family helped their relationship blossom, with the "incredible" Queen and "fantastically supportive" Duchess of Cambridge helping her settle in.

"This beautiful woman just tripped and fell into my life," said Harry. "We're a fantastic team, we know we are and over time we hope to have as much impact as possible." Set up by a mutual female friend, whom the couple declined to name, the Prince and a then-stranger were persuaded onto a blind date. Meghan, who claimed to know little about the Royal Family, asked nothing of the man she was being set up with, other than, "is he nice?"

"Because I'm from the States you don't grow up with the same understanding of the Royal Family," she said. "And so, while I now understand very clearly there is a global interest there, I didn't know much about him and so the only thing that I had asked her when she said she wanted to set us up was, 'Well, is he nice?' Because if he wasn't kind it just didn't seem like it would make sense."

Harry, too, knew little about his blind date, having never watched the television show *Suits* that Meghan starred in. "I'd never even heard of her," he said. "I was beautifully surprised when I walked into that room and saw her sitting there. I was like, wow, I really have done well, I've got to up my game."

After one date, Harry immediately asked to see her again the following day. "And then it was like, right,

diaries," he said. "We need to get the diaries out and find out how we're going to make this work, because I was off to Africa for a month, she was working. And we just said right where's the gap? And the gap happened to be in the perfect place."

From then on, their love blossomed. They spent time with "cosy nights in in front of the television, cooking dinner in our little cottage", said Harry. "It's made us a hell of a lot closer in a short space of time. For us, it's an opportunity for really getting to know each other without people looking or trying to take photos on their phones."

While hidden away in Nottingham Cottage, they spent time with William and Catherine, as well as taking tea with the Prince of Wales and the Queen. "William was longing to meet her and so was Catherine, so, you know, being our neighbours we managed to get that in quite a few times," said Harry. "Catherine has been absolutely amazing, as has William as well, you know, fantastic support."

"Just to take the time to be able to go on long country walks and just talk," said Meghan, who said the relationship had not felt like a whirlwind to them. "I think we were able to really have so much time just to connect and we never went longer than two weeks without seeing each other, even though we were obviously doing a long-distance relationship. So we made it work."

THE PROPOSAL

Harry's proposal came after an evening of domestic bliss. "Just a cosy night," said Meghan, in which they were "trying" to roast a chicken. "It was just an amazing surprise, it was so sweet and natural and very romantic. He got on one knee."

"

The fact that I fell in love
with Meghan so incredibly
quickly was confirmation
to me that all the stars
have aligned

"

Opposite: The newly engaged couple depart hand in hand

Asked whether she had said "yes" immediately, she told the Prince: "As a matter of fact, I could barely let you finish proposing, I said, 'Can I say yes now?'"

Harry confirmed this. "She didn't even let me finish. She said, 'can I say yes, can I say yes?' and then there were hugs. I had the ring in my finger and I was like 'can I give you the ring?' She goes 'oh yes, the ring'. So, no it was a really nice moment, it was just the two of us and I think I managed to catch her by surprise as well."

FAMILY SUPPORT

As this was before the birth of the Duke and Duchess of Cambridge's third child and Harry was fifth in line to the throne at the time, Her Majesty The Queen had to give her formal blessing for the marriage to take place. Harry said she was "delighted" and the Prince of Wales invited Meghan for tea. Harry's aunts on the Spencer side, to whom he has remained close, also spent time with the happy couple.

Harry expressed his surprise that his girlfriend was able to win over the Queen's corgis when she met his grandmother. He revealed that the normally snappy dogs sat happily at her feet during tea. "The corgis took to you straight away," said Harry. "I've spent the last 33 years being barked at; this one walks in, absolutely nothing. Just wagging tails and I was just like 'argh'."

Meghan said she had met the Queen several times and said it was "incredible" to get to know her through her grandson's eyes. "It's incredible to be able to meet her through his lens," she said, "not just with his honour and respect for her as the monarch, but the love that he has for her as his grandmother. All of those layers have been so important for me, so that when I met her I had such a deep understanding and, of course, incredible respect for being able to have that time with her. She's an incredible woman."

Harry added: "The family together have been absolutely a solid support. My grandparents, as well, have been wonderful throughout this whole process and they've known for quite some time. So how they haven't told anybody is again a miracle in itself. But now the whole family have come together and have been a huge amount of support."

The Prince also told of his meetings with his future mother-in-law, saying she was "amazing". He is yet to meet Ms Markle's father, Thomas, but has spoken to him on the telephone and did ask for permission to marry his daughter.

As a mixed-race woman, Ms Markle said, she had found some of the reaction to her ethnicity "disheartening". "It's a shame that that is the climate in this world to focus on a matter that's discriminatory," she said. "But I think, at the end of the day, I'm really just proud of who I am and where I come from." Her parents and close friends, she said, were a little concerned by her new-found public image, but were quickly won over after realising "they also had never seen me so happy".

"I know that I'm in love with this girl and I hope that she's in love with me," Prince Harry said, of the moment he realised she would be taking on a "media storm". "But we still had to sit down on the sofa and have some pretty frank conversations to say, 'what you're letting yourself in for is a big deal and it's not easy for anybody'. At the end of the day, she chooses me and I choose her and, whatever we have to tackle, it will be us together as a team. She's capable of anything and together there's a hell of a lot of work that needs doing.

"The fact that I know she will be unbelievably good at the job part of it as well is obviously a huge relief to me," continued Harry. "For me, it's an added member of the family. It's another team player as part of the bigger team. Both of us have passions for wanting to make change for good. With lots of young people running around the Commonwealth, that's where we want to spend most of our time. There's a lot to do."

Chapter Three

THE MAKING OF A PRINCE

Recovering from the heartbreak of
his mother's death when he was only
12, Harry grew up as the eccentric,
fiercely independent prince who
matured during army service

He is the flame-haired prince who captured the heart of the nation: the broken little boy walking behind the coffin of his late mother, Princess Diana. He has made the journey from royal teen rebel to courageous front-line soldier to much loved "people's prince".

Now, at last, he has found "the one". He said he had to "up his game" to woo Meghan and make her his wife. "I was beautifully surprised when I walked into that room and saw her," said Prince Harry. "I thought I'm really gonna have to up my game, sit down and make sure I have good chat."

He claimed he had never even heard of the famous TV star until this friend filled him in on the background. "I'd never watched any of Suits," he said during his engagement interview. Likewise, his status as a prince didn't faze her. She was only interested in his personality.

Luckily for Harry he has a big, warm personality. He has never traded on his royal rank but has been embraced and accepted for who he is and what he believes in. His has been quite an emotional journey of great highs and terrible lows – and it is the courage with which he has faced adversity that has made him one of the most popular royals.

Who can forget the images of the traumatised 12-year-old, with his head bowed and fists clenched, as he marched in the solemn funeral procession behind his late mother's coffin? Devastated Harry –along with his older brother, William; his father, The Prince of Wales; his grandfather, the Duke of Edinburgh; and his maternal uncle, Charles Spencer – all walked slowly through the heart of London on 6 September, 1997, watched by millions around the world.

Seven days earlier, his beautiful, charismatic mother Diana, Princess of Wales had died in a car crash in Paris, aged just 36. The world mourned the loss of the "People's Princess" but nobody could feel her loss more than Harry and William.

Placed on top of the coffin that day was a card to her. It read "Mummy". It is one of the most poignant images of mourning in modern times and perhaps one of the most distressing.

Her funeral, Harry later recalled, had overwhelmed him. He couldn't take in that she had died. "I don't think any child should be asked to do that, under any circumstances," he said later. "I don't think it would happen today." But brave and dutiful – and not wanting to let anyone down, least of all her – the little boy did what was asked of him, no realising the damage it was doing to him in the long term.

He had always been a mischievous, but happy little boy. A good skier, he would revel in skiing passed unsteady photographers on the slopes and knocking them over. He loved nothing more than to "play" fight with his Scotland Yard protection officers or dress up in children's army fatigues and play at being a real soldier.

He loved it when he outscored his older brother when he was taken by his mother to fire real guns at

Scotland Yard's firearms training unit at Lippitts Hill in Essex. Even as a youngster he was extremely proficient. He was always a cheeky boy, happy to face being admonished by his mother for poking his tongue out at the press. His nanny would pin him up against the wall with her tummy if he misbehaved.

PAINFUL RUMOURS

He has long been dogged by one particularly malicious false claim: after his mother openly spoke of her affair with Major James Hewitt, the rumour grew that it was the red-haired soldier and not Charles who was Harry's biological father. The claims are, of course, total rubbish – Diana had not even met Hewitt by the time Harry was born. Besides, early photographs of the young Prince Philip show that Harry also bears an uncanny resemblance to his paternal grandfather.

"These rumours of Harry's paternity angered Diana greatly," said Diana's bodyguard Inspector Wharfe MVO. "They were deeply cruel. She would say to me that Prince Charles was definitely Harry's father, of that she had no doubt." But the rumours persist to this day, even 20 years after her death.

Harry has survived personal "scandals" – with the public always forgiving him due to his likeability and willingness to admit his mistakes when he messed up. As a young boy he

was – according to those who knew him best – a handful. Full of life. At the age of seven, Prince Harry was like any other cheeky young boy, despite his privileged upbringing.

Diana was always determined that he and William would experience "normal life" as they were growing up in London – including using public transport. But that didn't always go to plan. One day in April 1992 instead of being chauffeur-driven to Smollensky's restaurant on The Strand for a family meal, Diana, William and Harry and their policeman got on a red London Routemaster bus. Harry revelled in being naughty.

Diana's Scotland Yard Protection Officer Inspector Ken Wharfe recalled: "Our driver was a Pakistani and, every time we set off after a stop, Harry couldn't resist tilting his head and saying loud and fast, and with a slight accent, 'Bud bud, ding ding!' within earshot of the other passengers and, indeed, the driver." Diana immediately scolded Harry. She was "furious" with his behaviour.

Harry was not deterred and ignored the ticking off by bus mother. Instead, relentlessly, he continued making the comment every time the bell was rung for a stop. They all got off at the next stop. The next day, under instructions from his disappointed mother, Harry wrote to the policeman and thanked him for arranging his trip. He signed off, "Bud bud ding ding, Harry." It was a demonstration of his fierce independence.

Left: Charles, William and Harry look at the floral tributes to Diana, Princess of Wales at Kensington Palace

TEENAGE KICKS

As a teenager he dabbled in drink and drugs that embarrassed his family. He went to a fancy dress party dressed as a Nazi, which caused uproar. But it was his time in the army – where he served two tours of duty in Afghanistan – that made the man. Even when serving, however in August 2012, he became the subject of numerous news stories after nude photos of the royal had been leaked to the public.

The images of the prince were taken during a private party in a hotel room in Las Vegas where the prince had been vacationing. He and his friends had reportedly been playing a game of strip billiards. The photos of the partying prince ran in the tabloid *Sun* newspaper, but most other papers declined to run them.

Within days, however, he was posted to Afghanistan to serve again and while the story dominated the headlines for a short time, the scandal seems had no lasting impact on his popular public image.

One of his first public appearances after the Las Vegas incident was at the WellChild Awards in London, where he received a warm welcome.

Harry, who serves as a patron to WellChild, a charity that is dedicated to supporting sick children and their families, even joked in his speech that he was "never shy

"

*Since leaving the army –
where he felt most at home
among the officers and
NCOs who served under
him – in 2015 he has thrown
himself into charity work*

"

Chapter Four

THE PRINCE'S BRIDE

Born in California to a white father
and a black mother, the American
actress Meghan Markle has proved her
worth as a feminist, an ambassador
and a humanitarian

As a little girl Meghan recalled her confusion when asked about her ethnicity. At the age of seven she was asked to tick a box confirming her ethnicity, but there was nothing for a mixed-race child. Rather than choosing between "black" or "white" she left it blank, despite the fact that her teacher advised her to tick "white" given she had light-coloured skin. When she told her father, Thomas Markle, he was enraged. But, with all the good will in the world, Thomas Markle (who is of Dutch-Irish ancestry) and his wife Doria (who is African-American) were never going to be able to shield their beautiful bi-racial daughter from prejudice. His response was absolute. "If it happens again," he told his daughter, "you draw your own box."

It was something that would live with the determined little girl through to adulthood. She was deeply proud of her roots – both black and white. She would later write and talk with pride of her ancestry. In an article she penned for *Elle* magazine Meghan openly discussed her bi-racial heritage. She explained that in 1865, when slavery was abolished in the United States, former slaves had to choose their own surname and her great-great-great grandfather called himself "Wisdom". "While my mixed heritage may have created a grey area surrounding my self-identification, keeping me with a foot on both sides of the fence, I have come to embrace that," she wrote. "To say who I am, to share where I'm from, to voice my pride in being a strong, confident mixed-race woman."

MOTHER LOVE

Meghan has also talked warmly of her close relationship with her "free spirited" mother, Doria Ragland, a yoga instructor and social worker who works as a clinical therapist with the geriatric community. "She's got dread locks and a nose ring," Meghan told *Glamour* magazine. "She just ran the LA Marathon. We can just have so much fun together, and yet I'll still find so much solace in her support. That duality coexists the same way it would in a best friend."

Her parents had met in the late 1970s when her father Thomas (who already had two children, Samantha

*Left: Meghan speaks up at the
One Young World Summit*

and Thomas, Jr. from a previous relationship) was working as a lighting director for a popular soap opera and her mother was temping at the studio. "I like to think he was drawn to her sweet eyes and her Afro, plus their shared love of antiques," Meghan wrote. Whatever it was, they married and had Meghan. She was born 4 August 1981 in Los Angeles, California and named Rachel by her parents (Meghan was her second name). They moved to The Valley, an area of L.A. which was "leafy and affordable", says Markle. "What it was not, however, was diverse. And there was my mom, caramel in complexion with her light-skinned baby in tow, being asked where my mother was since they assumed she was the nanny."

She was six years old when her parents split, and Meghan lived with her mother although she would regularly visit her father. The View Park-Windsor Hills neighbourhood in which she grew up with her mother has been described as "the black Beverly Hills" with the median price of a home there being $771,000. She attended a private primary school before studying at a girls' Roman Catholic college and later graduating from Northwestern University School of Communication in 2003, the first member of her family to do so, just as her acting career was beginning.

She graduated with a double major in theatre and international relations. She said she wanted to be an actor, but wanted more than that too, not wanting to be a cliche.

"

Meghan has talked warmly of her close relationship with her 'free spirited' mother, Doria Ragland

"

Left: Pictured with Suits co-star Patrick J Adams

For a while, in her early twenties, it looked as if she would pursue a career as a diplomat instead. She applied and got an internship with the US State Department and was rewarded with a stint at the US Embassy in Buenos Aires, Argentina for a few months.

AN ACTING CAREER

But Meghan had got the drama bug as was determined to follow her dream. At school she had shown great talent and it developed while she was a university. Her career started slowly at first. Her first role came in a soap opera *General Hospital* in 2002 before moving on to roles in *CSI*, *Without a Trace* and *Castle*.

Between auditions, she has told of making money by doing calligraphy for wedding invitations, using skills developed in handwriting classes at school. Her agent then managed to secure her roles in major Hollywood films, including *Get Him to the Greek*, *Remember Me* and *Horrible Bosses*. She also appeared in the sci-fi series *Fringe*, playing FBI special agent Amy Jessup.

However, it was the US legal drama *Suits* – shown on the USA network in the States and on the Dave channel and Netflix in the UK – that saw her achieve global fame and financial security. She plays the ambitious, determined paralegal Rachel Zane who is also the girlfriend of the fraudulent lawyer and central character Mike Ross, played by Patrick J. Adams. *Suits* is set in New York City but filmed in Toronto, and Markle lived in a rented house in the Canadian city's Seaton Village neighbourhood while the series was filmed. She starred in the show from its launch in 2011 to the end of the seventh series in November 2017.

Around this time the show launched, in September 2011, she married film producer Trevor Engelson in Jamaica. The couple has been dating for a while before they wed but the difficulties of them living and working in different cities took its toll and sadly they divorced two years later.

A CAMPAIGNING VOICE

Meghan also became a United Nations women's advocate (for Political Participation and Leadership) and publicly supported actress Emma Watson's He For She campaign. In 2015, she narrated a public service announcement for the organisation and has given a speech before the UN Secretary General Ban Ki Moon. As she says in a blog post: "I've never wanted to be a lady who lunches – I've always wanted to be a woman who works."

Meghan is also an ardent feminist, something that dates back to childhood. Aged 11 she made her TV debut, appearing on the Nickelodeon show *Nick News with Linda Ellerbee* to register her annoyance at an advertisement for washing-up liquid with the gender-specific tagline "Women all over America are fighting greasy pots and pans". She wrote to women's rights lawyer Gloria Allred and the then First Lady Hillary Clinton to protest against this tagline, and Allred and Clinton apparently pledged

their support. Months later the advert was changed to: "*People* all over America are fighting greasy pots and pans."

In February 2016 she was made an ambassador for Canada's World Vision Clean Water campaign and, as part of that role, she has travelled to Rwanda. She was seen talking to Canadian Prime Minister Justin Trudeau at the One Young World Summit in Ottawa, a celebration of young leaders from across the world.

She also ran her own her own lifestyle website and brand called "TheTig.com" which covered topics such as food, beauty, fashion and travel and also spoke about strong women. She said she set it up reframe the beauty content to include think pieces about self-empowerment and feature dynamic, inspirational women. In this time she developed a large social network following, with 1.9 million people following her posts on Instagram and over 350,000 Twitter followers. But after three years she closed it – in April 2017 – leading to frenzied speculation that she was preparing for a royal engagement.

Commenting on how she managed to combine her acting career with her humanitarian commitments, she said: "While my life shifts from refugee camps to red carpets, I choose them both because these worlds can, in fact, co-exist. And for me, they must."

Chapter Five

THE SECRET ROMANCE

Harry and Meghan managed to keep their relationship under wraps for six months before the official announcement that put the couple well and truly in the spotlight

"

One of the most famous
and eligible men on the
planet managed to keep
his relationship secret for
nearly half a year before
the news broke

"

Chapter Six

A ROYAL CHRISTMAS

Christmas day spent with the
royals at Sandringham saw
Meghan warmly welcomed by
the Windsors, who she described
as "the big family I never had"

Wearing a camel wraparound coat paired with a fancy chestnut hat and Stuart Weitzman boots, Meghan Markle walked arm-in-arm with her fiancé Prince Harry as they made the short journey from Sandringham House to St Mary Magdalene Church for the early-morning service on Christmas Day.

If she was nervous, she certainly did not show it. She seemed at ease, despite being at the heart of the Royal Family for the first time, joining in as they smiled and politely chatted with loyal members of the public who had waited for hours to see them. Meghan stayed close to Harry, watched him work the crowd as he had done for years, and followed his lead.

The pair walked alongside the Duke and Duchess of Cambridge, so often the centre of attention as far as the royal fans were concerned. However, this time, William and Kate were happy to pass on the attention to Harry and Meghan. The next day, a candid photograph of the two couples beaming appeared in newspapers around the world, and the quartet were quickly dubbed "the fab four". The image was not taken by a professional photographer but by single mother Karen Anvil, 39, from Watlington, Norfolk, who was among the dozens of well-wishers who gathered to catch a glimpse of the royals.

The main residence on the 20,000-acre Sandringham Estate is actually smaller than most of the other royal residences, so only the Queen's closest family usually

"

She wants to spend
this time learning about
the UK, getting to
know this country and
travelling around the
Commonwealth

"

be a moment of "fun and joy". Knauf added that Windsor was a "very special place" for the Prince, and that he and Meghan had regularly spent time there together during their 16-month romance.

He also revealed that she would be giving up her charitable roles in order to start her royal life with a "clean slate". The American actress, who previously worked with World Vision Canada and as a UN women's advocate, stepped away from her commitments to focus on her preparations for royal life.

"She wants to spend this time learning about the UK," said Knauf. "She has made the decision that she wants to start with a clean slate and focus on the UK, and getting to know this country, and travelling around the Commonwealth. So, the only role that she will begin with is as patron of the Royal Foundation. That has been a decision that she has taken. This is the country that's going to be her home now and that means travelling around, getting to know the towns and cities and smaller communities."

Journalists in the room were surprised when he said the introduction to the UK would begin straight away with an "away day" visit to Nottingham in the same week that the couple's nuptials were announced. Meghan, now a trainee royal, decided she wanted to hit the ground running.

Chapter Seven

"HI, I'M MEGHAN"

Harry and Meghan followed the
announcement of their engagement
with a nationwide meet-and-greet tour,
introducing the glamorous bride-to-be
to well-wishers throughout the
United Kingdom

After more than a year of preserving their privacy, the prince and his US actress girlfriend decided to take their relationship to the next level by going public. The moment came with their first ever joint public appearance at the third Invictus Games, the international multi-sport event that Prince Harry created for wounded, injured or sick armed services personnel. Harry launched the games in London in March 2014, took them to Florida in May 2016, and then to Toronto in September 2017.

At the opening ceremony for the Toronto games, Meghan may have sat separately from Harry under the watchful eye of a protection officer but it was a significant sign of how serious their relationship was. Later in the week, they attended the tennis together in a surprise appearance in front of the cameras. The cat was now well and truly out of the bag.

By the time the Invictus Games had come to an end the couple were happy to go public. They were not shy around each other. They joined Meghan's mother, Doria Ragland, in a suite at the Air Canada Centre for the closing ceremony. They were reportedly "snuggling, kissing, with their arms around each other".

Harry reportedly left his official seat after the ceremony began and went to the seats occupied by Meghan, Doria, Jessica Mulroney (daughter-in-law of the former Canadian Prime Minister Brian Mulroney) and Markus Anderson (the Canadian who introduced

Previous pages: A happy Harry and Meghan enjoy their first public walkabout in Nottingham

Left: The Prince and his fiancée visit Cardiff Castle

Meghan and Harry). Meghan even wore a white shirt, made by the American fashion designer Misha Nonoo, called "The Husband" – a name that got the media tongues wagging. Perhaps, the travelling press pack concluded, an announcement of a royal wedding wasn't that far off.

Harry chatted openly about his girlfriend, as well. He said that Meghan Markle was "loving" the Invictus Games after she attended the wheelchair tennis hand-in-hand with him. It was the first time that Prince Harry had spoken publicly and freely about Meghan, following the written statement released by Kensington Palace that confirmed their relationship. As far as the press were concerned the countdown to the royal wedding had started. They were not wrong.

THE ANNOUNCEMENT

A series of stories followed. Meghan giving up her social media platforms, talk of her negotiating her exit from the hugely successful drama *Suits*, stories of romantic holidays in Norway and Botswana, and her attendance at the wedding of the Duchess of Cambridge's sister, Pippa Middleton, all stoked the rumour fire.

Then it emerged that Harry had taken his girlfriend to formally meet the Queen at the Palace to get her blessing for the marriage, something he was obliged to ask for under the Succession to the Crown Act 2013. Her Majesty gave her permission willingly, thrilled that at last her grandson, with whom she is very close, had found the one he could share his life with.

Finally, after another weekend of frenzied media speculation, the official announcement came from Clarence House, Prince Charles's office, on Monday 27 November.

It did not come as any surprise to the media or the public, but what did was the speed with which this royal bride-to-be would get to work. Within days she was on her way to Nottingham with Harry at her side for the first of several trips around the UK to familiarise herself with the country that would be her new home. Within a few months of the engagement announcement, Harry and Meghan had toured around the United Kingdom, visiting every country in the Queen's realm, taking in Nottingham, Brixton in south London, Edinburgh, Cardiff and Belfast.

It was quite an education for the Californian actress, meeting thousands of people, shaking thousands of hands and making small talk with complete strangers, but she took it in her stride. Often not waiting for Harry to show her the way, she would introduce herself with a cheery "Hi, I'm Meghan." As she worked the line of well-wishers behind the steel security barriers during a walkabout she would add, "I'm so happy, it's just such a thrill to be here."

"

It was quite an education for the Californian actress, shaking thousands of hands and making small talk with complete strangers, but she took it in her stride

"

Right: The bride-to-be chatted to local children and showed them her engagement ring on the Welsh leg of the royal couple's tour

event to mark World Aids Day. Dominic Edwards, from the Terrence Higgins Trust, a charity supported by Harry's late mother Princess Diana, said the charity was "thrilled" that the couple had chosen to visit Nottingham and the Terrence Higgins Trust event. "I think it really underlines his great support for HIV as a cause."

THE TOUR CONTINUES

The couples' next stop a few days later was multicultural Brixton in south London, where they met presenters at Reprezent 107.3 FM – the only UK radio station presented solely by young people. They listened intently as they were told how the station trains hundreds of young people each year in media and employment skills. As they arrived, fans began chanting, "I love you Meghan." The small crowd didn't even shout for Harry, something he would have to get used to. She seemed overwhelmed when she got out the car and kept turning towards the crowd causing a hysterical reaction. Harry tapped her on her shoulder to advise her to turn away.

Inside, fittingly, the pair listened to the track "Flirt" by the artist Poté. Meghan praised teenage presenter Gloria Beyi, 17, telling her: "I can see why your show is so popular. You're so thoughtful and your approach is so engaging." Harry told the station's founder, Shane Carey, 46, the work he was doing was "amazing", while Meghan made everyone laugh when she told them: "I must tune in."

Afterwards, they greeted well-wishers who had waited for hours in the freezing cold and even stopped to pose for selfies. Foster carer Sharley Watson, 55, waited

Chapter Eight

THE FAB FOUR

Together with William and Kate,
Harry and Meghan make up an
impressive foursome – and a fine
ambassadorial team for their
Royal Foundation

" Meghan is a mature
woman with a voice
and she is clearly not
afraid to use it
"

wait a couple of months and then we can hit the ground running. We can multitask, that's fine!"

The foursome also poked fun at the perils of working together. "Working as a family does have its challenges, of course it does," Prince Harry said, to laughter. "We're stuck together forever now!"

Meghan said they each brought their own perspectives to issues. "If everyone's thinking the same way," she said, "how are you going to push the envelope, how are you really going to break through in a different sort of mindset?" It was an accomplished performance from an accomplished actress.

PUBLIC AFFECTION

A few days later, Harry and Meghan were on the road again. In Birmingham in early March they seemed much more at ease working together in public. They appeared to be getting the hang of it.

They were very tactile publicly, much more than William and Kate ever are. While Harry and Meghan had previously been seen holding hands and grasping arms, on this "away-day" visit to the Midlands they displayed more intimate gestures, playful pats and

Previous pages and below: Harry and
Meghan have not been afraid to show
public displays of affection, as they
did on their visit to Birmingham earlier
in the year

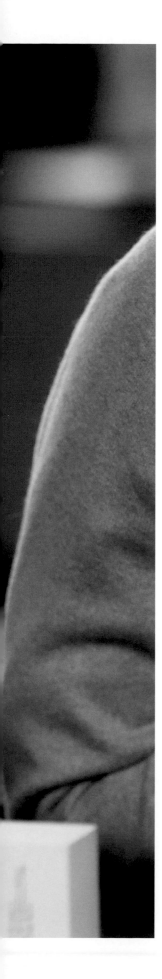

hands on the smalls of each other's backs. It was as if they were almost oblivious to the crowds around them. This newfound confidence was reflected in the way they interacted with the crowd too. Schoolgirl Sophia Richards, 10, got closer than most to Meghan after she was swept into an impromptu embrace with the future royal.

The couple were there to celebrate the aspirations of young women on International Women's Day and, despite enduring a wait in the drizzling rain, enthusiastic locals cheered and waved Union Flags as they finally caught sight of the royal pair, who stopped to speak to onlookers as they made their way to Millennium Point. Meghan – dressed in a coat by J.Crew, trousers by Alexander Wang and an AllSaints jumper – was greeted by shouts of "You're beautiful!"

While in the city, they attended an event encouraging young women to pursue careers in science, technology, engineering and maths (STEM). Hosted by social enterprise "Stemettes", the event saw the couple speak to students about the challenges of working in male-dominated STEM industries.

The pair donned headsets resembling a virtual-reality rollercoaster. Meghan said she was shocked by some of the technology on display, including pianos made out of bananas and how to "hack the web". She told some students that the coding they were working on looked very impressive, saying: "Wow, that's really cool."

FAMILY PLANS?

On their fifth away-day – an unannounced visit to Northern Ireland – Meghan dropped a huge baby hint. She made it clear that she and Harry are already thinking about starting a family during a visit to a science park. She gestured at an array of baby equipment and said: "I am sure at one point we will need the whole thing."

The couple were eager to find out about the latest products for new parents and their infants when they were shown items produced by Shnuggle, a firm that makes innovative baby products, including a baby bath that enables the baby to sit up, a changing mat and a Moses basket.

"It's very sweet," said Meghan. Sinead Murphy, who founded the company with her husband Adam, said: "They seemed very engaged with the products. Harry was particularly interested in the bath. I wonder if he has witnessed bath time with his nephew or niece. As soon as he saw the bum bump [which stops the baby slipping down] he understood immediately. He said, 'Oh, non-slip'."

Asked to interpret Meghan's baby hint, she said: "With an upcoming marriage it's likely there is going to be an announcement in the next few years."

Harry himself dropped a big hint in November during the engagement interview that babies will be on the horizon soon. When asked, "Children?" Harry replied drily: "Not currently no," and then added: "One step at a time and hopefully we'll start a family in the near future."

Chapter Nine

THE FUTURE

One of Harry and Meghan's main roles in
the future is likely to be as "super envoys"
for the Commonwealth, continuing the
invaluable service the Queen has done
for more than 60 years

Previous pages and left:
The royals attend the
Commonwealth Day service
at Westminster Abbey

of royals – including Meghan – to understand it and serve it with equal dedication. Harry and Meghan had already spoken of their passion for the Commonwealth cause, using their engagement interview to spell out their hopes for engaging with its young people.

A FINE PERFORMANCE

If Meghan looked a little nervous at first it was understandable. After being invited to join the Queen at one of the most important events of her year, she was keen to make a good impression. The former actress, who has undertaken to become a British citizen, appeared to have been doing some research ahead of her first official engagement alongside Her Majesty, a major milestone for the bride-to-be.

She confidently joined in with the national anthem, paying respect to her future grandmother-in-law, faultlessly singing "God Save The Queen" and two hymns, "Lord Of All Hopefulness" and "Guide Me, O Thou Great Redeemer" with gusto.

The service saw the Royal Family out in force, with the Prince of Wales, the Duchess of Cornwall, the Duke of York, the Princess Royal and the Countess of Wessex among those supporting the Queen and showing their own enthusiasm for the "Commonwealth connection".

Prince William, Kate, Harry and Meghan arrived at the service – which boasted a 2,000-strong congregation – together, taking prominent seats for the televised spectacle. Wearing a cream dress and coat by Amanda Wakeley and beret by Stephen Jones, Ms Markle was cheered by waiting crowds as she stepped out of her car at Westminster Abbey, joining William and Kate to watch a performance from drummers before stepping inside.

During the service, the Prime Minister, Theresa May, gave a Bible reading, Portsmouth Gospel Choir sang "Bridge Over Troubled Water" and Dr Andrew Bastawrous, an eye surgeon who has turned a smartphone into an examination tool to combat avoidable blindness in developing countries, gave the reflection.

The congregation included major Commonwealth figures including the Prime Minister of Malta Joseph Muscat, Commonwealth Secretary-General Baroness Scotland, high commissioners, ambassadors, senior politicians from across the UK and Commonwealth, faith leaders and more than 800 schoolchildren and young people.

"The service was beautiful," Meghan told a visiting teacher, "especially the choir and the music. It was great to see people from all over the world so well represented at the service." She also admitted that

"

*The Commonwealth
will be the Queen's legacy
and she expects the next
generation of royals to
understand it and serve
it with equal dedication*

"

Opposite: Harry and Meghan will
play key roles as ambassadors for
Britain on the international stage

she was "very, very excited" when asked about her
fast-approaching wedding.

AN INTERNATIONAL ROLE

During her research into the Royal Family, the importance
of events such as the Commonwealth Day service would
have been impressed upon Meghan. The Royal Family is,
after all, a working family – working for the institution
of the monarchy in the service of its people.

It is clear that the Queen, who is always personally
debriefed by members of her family after overseas
Commonwealth visits they have undertaken on her
behalf, plans to use the new royal "power couple" as
Commonwealth super envoys.

Following their wedding, Harry and Meghan are
expecting to be set to work on major foreign forays to
Canada, Australia and New Zealand in the same year.
Another key destination for them to visit is India as well
as the Commonwealth nations in Africa, but that is not
expected until 2019.

The Queen and the now retired Prince Philip, 96,
no longer undertake long-haul travel and Her Majesty
wants to capitalise on the popularity of her grandson
and his bride to cement ties and help smooth the path
for trade deals with key Commonwealth nations.

The couple even made a point of mentioning going
around the Commonwealth in their BBC engagement
interview. "There's a lot to do," they both agreed. They
are expected to add to that a royal tour of other areas
of Australia, as well as possibly a trip to neighbouring
New Zealand later this year. A Foreign Office source
confirmed plans are already in the pipeline.

The royals play a key "soft power" role in helping
Britain to negotiate new trade agreements. In trade
and diplomatic terms, royal visits pack a formidable
soft-power punch. The Queen hosted the Commonwealth
Heads of Government Meeting this April in London and
Windsor. Again Harry and Meghan played highly visible
roles. These will be roles that they will play on the world
stage for the rest of their lives.

Chapter Ten

A REGAL SETTING

St George's Chapel, in the grounds of
Windsor Castle, is steeped in royal history,
both as a resting place for monarchs and
the site of many royal weddings

S t George's Chapel, Windsor, the venue of Harry and Meghan's wedding, has hosted more than a dozen royal weddings; from the pomp and pageantry of the ceremony of future King/Emperor Edward VII's to Princess Alexandra of Denmark in 1863 to the low-key nuptials of the Queen Elizabeth's oldest grandson, Peter Phillips to Autumn Kelly in 2008.

The chapel, a "Royal Peculiar" which is under the direct jurisdiction of the monarch, is deeply rooted in history and tradition. As well as being the site of the Order of the Garter, the most senior order of British Chivalry, established in 1348 by Edward III, it is also where several royals are buried.

Within it there are tombs of 10 monarchs, including Henry VIII, Charles I, Edward IV, Edward VII, George III, George IV, William IV and George V. The Queen's parents – George VI and Queen Elizabeth, the Queen Mother – were also laid to rest there, as was her younger sister, Princess Margaret. It is the planned burial site for the Queen herself.

BEAUTIFUL WINDSOR

Harry and Meghan chose Windsor as it is very special to them. They regularly spent time there as their relationship developed and said they are "delighted that the beautiful grounds" of the castle will be where they begin their lives as a married couple.

*Left: Prince Charles and the
Duchess of Cornwall walk
from St George's Chapel
after their blessing and civil
wedding in 2005*

A service of "Prayer and Dedication" for Prince
Charles's marriage to Camilla Parker Bowles was the last
wedding service to take place there in April 2005. It
immediately followed a civil ceremony at Windsor Guildhall.

The Queen, who did not attend the civil service but
was at the blessing, hosted a reception for her son and
new daughter-in-law. Passionate about horse racing and
noting that the wedding date coincided with the Grand
National, in which she had a horse running, Her Majesty
began her speech by saying she had two important
announcements to make. The first was that Hedgehunter
had won the race at Aintree; the second was that, at
Windsor, she was delighted to be welcoming her son
and his bride to the "winners enclosure". "They have
overcome Becher's Brook and The Chair and all kinds
of other terrible obstacles," she said. "They have come
through and I'm very proud and wish them well. My son
is home and dry with the woman he loves."

At the reception, in the state apartments, Charles
too gave a touching speech in which he thanked "my
dear mama" for footing the bill and "my darling Camilla,
who has stood with me through thick and thin and whose
precious optimism and humour have seen me through".

Queen Elizabeth's youngest son, Prince Edward,
married Sophie Rhys-Jones on June 19, 1999, at St George's

"

Harry and Meghan chose Windsor as it is very special to them. They regularly spent time there as their relationship developed

"

Left: Peter Phillips and
Autumn Kelly wed at
St George's in 2008

Twenty-two years after her parents were married at St George's Chapel, Princess Alice Mary of Albany married Prince Alexander of Teck at the same venue on February 10, 1904. Because the Duke of Albany died prematurely of haemophilia, Princess Alice's uncle, King Edward VII, walked her down the aisle and hosted a 14-course banquet for her afterward at St George's Hall at Windsor Castle.

Another granddaughter of Queen Victoria, Princess Margaret of Connaught, married the future King Gustaf VI Adolf of Sweden at St George's Chapel on June 15, 1905. The banquet that followed featured two dishes to honour the heir to the Swedish throne, including Zèphires de Crabes á la Suédoise – named after Sweden – and Chaufroix de Cailles à la Bernadotte – named after the Bernadotte house to which the Swedish royal family belongs.

While a niece of Queen Mary was married at St George's in 1919, the next royal wedding to happen at Windsor Castle didn't take place until December 14, 1957, when Queen Elizabeth II's cousin, Anne Abel Smith, married David Liddell-Grainger in a televised event.

Every aspect of Harry and Meghan's wedding was covered by the cameras too, pulling in an estimated global television audience of two billion, matching that of Prince Harry's brother William's wedding to Kate Middleton on 29 April 2011 at Westminster Abbey.

Chapter Eleven

WEALTH, HEALTH & HAPPINESS

ROCK SOLID INVESTMENTS

BENTLEY INVESTMENTS

Bentley Investments is one of Gibraltar's major real-estate players, with a clear vision for the future. "We want to raise the bar for property development in Gibraltar and create a thriving year-round resort-style destination with no compromises," says Bentley Investments' Chairman Evgeny Cherepakhov. Bentley Investments develops, builds and manages property in this British Overseas Territory. It has a deep-rooted commitment to delivering exemplary levels of design, finish and servicing on its projects, which span residential, commercial and office spaces.

Cherepakhov moved to Gibraltar in the 1990s and quickly realised that there was an opportunity to cultivate a new breed of development, drawing upon global influences from not only the residential sector but high-end hotels and restaurants, for which service level is paramount. "We are creating aspirational developments for discerning individuals who don't have the time or desire to deal with day-to-day hassles," he says. "We have on-site management teams to ensure smooth running and, at our latest development, we are also introducing a 24/7 physical concierge and parcel room, the likes of which has not been seen here before."

As well as providing high-specification living accommodation, Bentley Investments' latest developments will also deliver outstanding amenities, along with commercial and retail space, creating vibrant destinations with high levels of kerb appeal. Providing contrast to many existing developments in Gibraltar, Cherepakhov wants to ensure that his developments integrate with the wider community.

At the forefront of this vision is the landmark EuroCity development,punctuated by three sustainable towers – one of which will be the tallest in Gibraltar. Designed by the award-winning UK-based architects the Manser Practice,

it will provide 366 homes set among beautifully landscaped podium gardens, with swathes of commercial and retail space that can be enjoyed by a wider audience.

"Many developments here are accessible only to residents, but we want to change this," says Cherepakhov. "While there will be a collection of resident-specific amenities, at ground level we are also providing space that is open to the public, with cafés, restaurants, shops and more. We want to ensure that everyone can enjoy and make use of our spaces, whether they are professionals, families or tourists."

Innovative technology forms the spine of each Bentley Investments project, allowing each development to deliver a truly world-class offering. "Technology has allowed us to create sustainable contemporary buildings with solar panels, water-saving systems and charging points for electric vehicles," says Cherepakhov. "Meanwhile, at the user end, we are rolling out a new concierge application for their smartphones that will allow residents to do everything from making restaurant bookings to ordering cleaning or maintenance services at the touch of a button. It is these little details that we introduce in our developments that set us apart."

Cherepakhov proudly describes Bentley Investments' developments as "one of a kind". "You live in a resort where you have beautiful weather," he says. "You have stunning design, you have gardens, you have pools, you have the Mediterranean climate. But you also don't have to leave behind the luxuries and the services that come with a global city. You've got everything you need at your doorstep, and everything you need at your fingertips."
www.bentley.gi

THE THOUGHT THAT ACCOUNTS

KPMG

From its earliest days, KPMG has maintained an enduring connection to the Royal Family. The relationship developed partly thanks to Sir Michael Peat, who was a partner at the accountancy firm of Peat Marwick when it merged with Klynveld Main Goerdeler to form KPMG in 1987. Sir Michael was administrative adviser to the Royal Household, before being appointed Keeper of the Privy Purse, Treasurer to Her Majesty The Queen and Receiver General of the Duchy of Lancaster and subsequently the Principal Private Secretary to His Royal Highness The Prince of Wales.

"We have a long and proud history of association with the Royal Family," says Rachel Hopcroft, Head of Corporate Affairs. Many of these connections are related to KPMG's commitment to social responsibility. "We place great importance on being a person-led organisation rather than simply a business. Obviously we need to be successful in what we do but it's also very important to think about community and how you create a wider social impact."

KPMG uses its position as one of Britain's leading professional services firms to support numerous initiatives. One example is Pitch@Palace, where KPMG was a founding partner. This initiative was started by the Duke of York to encourage young entrepreneurs, often from disadvantaged backgrounds, to present their business ideas at Buckingham Palace. In addition, the firm supports both the Prince's Trust and the Diana Award, mentoring young people from disadvantaged backgrounds to help them build the skills and aspirations needed for the world of work.

KPMG has over 14,500 partners and staff, spanning more than 20 offices in the UK. The firm places high importance on the impact it has in the communities in which it operates and has focused its corporate responsibility approach accordingly. "We try to align what we are doing with the more disadvantaged parts of the country, the places that the government calls 'social mobility coldspots'," says Hopcroft. "We really want to focus our attention on the places where the need is greater."

Hopcroft emphasises the importance of giving back to communities through skills-based volunteering. "We want our staff to use their skills," she says. "We are a highly skilled organisation and we want to use that in our community to make volunteering opportunities more impactful both for those giving their time and the people on the end of it."

This focus has led to KPMG contributing towards the set-up of The City Academy, Hackney ten years ago. "We are located in one of the most disadvantaged parts of London," says Hopcroft, "so we helped set up a school that is now recognised as one of the top 10 most improved schools in the country." KPMG volunteers provide a holistic programme of support to the school, which includes five positions on the board of governors, pro-bono support on financial management and work experience to broaden students' career horizons.

Last year, KPMG received The Queen's Award for Enterprise for Promoting Opportunity (through social mobility). It also came second in the first Social Mobility Employer Index, which recognises organisations that have embedded social mobility into their talent strategies. In addition, KPMG has been awarded for their leadership, commitment and mentoring at the inaugural UK Social Mobility Awards. "This belief in community comes from the very top," says Hopcroft, "and it's something we believe in very passionately."

www.kpmg.co.uk

PATENT GENIUSES

MINESOFT

"We're selling something that's helping people solve their problems around the world," says Ann Chapman-Daniel, co-founder and Managing Director of Minesoft. "It's a successful business, but I genuinely think it does help people to make progress."

Minesoft offers a service to inventors – research labs, big companies or tiny start-ups – who want to take out a patent. "Inventions start with an idea," says Chapman-Daniel. "And if that idea could be used in industry, then it tends to end up being filed as a patent, an intellectual property right, like a trademark."

When a company develops a new product, it needs to protect its intellectual property by filing a patent. To do so successfully – and to avoid the risk of litigation – it is essential to ensure that it is not infringing on any existing patents. Minesoft offers access to a searchable database of more than 100 million patent documents, updated every week with new additions, as well as a range of legal and competitive intelligence patent information solutions.

"PatBase is a massive database of scientific and technical innovation," says Chapman-Daniel. "Each of those documents individually will have technical drawings attached to them or chemical structures." The average patent document is about ten pages long, and some pharmaceutical or life-sciences patents run to thousands of pages.

"An industrial product such as a vacuum cleaner, for example, would be protected by a plethora of individual patents that protect various aspects of the product – it might be an electrical or mechanical component or a chemical material to make it faster or better in some respect."

Inventions are filed in long, complex patent documents, says Chapman-Daniel. "They have to give detailed descriptions of the technology and have a range of technical drawings so that an engineer or chemist understands what is being invented and what the technical innovation is."

This comprises much detail to search, which is where Minesoft's latest patent analytics landscaping service comes in handy. It can analyse up to a million patents in mere seconds, and allows users to personalise their own dashboards. "You can visualise what is in those patents according to the companies or inventors and the areas of technologies that they fall within," says Chapman-Daniel.

She and her husband, Ophir Daniel, founded Minesoft in 1996. The company is based in Richmond, west London, with offices in the USA, Germany and Japan and partners and distributors worldwide. "It's very international," says Chapman-Daniel. "If someone wants to file a patent, their patent attorney will need to check whether that idea has been thought of before, and if somebody else already owns the intellectual property right. That won't be just in your own country – and they're all in different languages."

Minesoft works with the World Intellectual Property Organization to give free or low-cost access to their global database, which benefits the poorest nations. "Gaining access to global IP and seeing what's been invented in other parts of the world to help with, say, irrigation or developing their own infrastructure is a tangible benefit," says Chapman-Daniel. "New business markets are also being found in China and Minesoft provides content in Chinese. An advantage lies in finding partners in the West who they could work with to develop their own technology – because if you own a patent, you own the intellectual property. Everywhere, all over the world, you find inventive people. We are privileged to be able to help them."
minesoft.com

CARE IN THE HOME

HOME INSTEAD SENIOR CARE

"We deliver relationship-led care," says Martin Jones, UK Managing Director of Home Instead Senior Care, "not purely functional or task-based care, which is unfortunately the norm in the sector. When my own father had prostate cancer and was being looked after in his home, I learned it was companionship that he wanted most from his caregiver – someone to watch TV with him or go to the shop."

This relationship-focused approach is the cornerstone of Home Instead's philosophy. It's why its caregivers are meticulously matched with its clients, and why typically no visit is ever less than an hour. "We view our clients as customers, not 'service users'," says Jones. "That's why we are the first and only UK care provider to be awarded the Queen's Award for Innovation, because we put our clients' wishes at the heart of everything we do."

Everything is tailored to whatever the client requires to stay happy and comfortable at home. Each care plan is personally designed according to the specifications of the client and their family, and could comprise anything from a couple of hours of companionship per week to ten hours a day for end-of-life care. Home Instead caregivers are non-medical, explains Jones, though they team up with district GPs and Macmillan nurses to provide comprehensive care for those who need it. "Home Instead caregivers can even accompany clients on holiday – we provide whatever the individual wants to maintain their independence and connections with society," says Jones. "Our caregivers act as a trusted friend and companion in every scenario. Many of our caregivers are also older, which is an advantage, as it means they have more life experience and are likely to share more common ground with our clients."

Caregivers join the business from a variety of professional backgrounds, such as retail and hospitality, and receive full training, which includes end of life training and City & Guilds-accredited dementia training, taking in the latest in Alzheimer's education and home-care techniques. Home Instead is the only UK care provider to have received the Princess Royal Training Award in recognition of the high standard of its training schemes.

"It's a very rewarding job," says Jones. "All of our caregivers want to give something back and support the client as much as they can. It's about having a caring attitude, empathy and wanting to make a difference."
www.homeinstead.co.uk

Chapter Twelve

THE PERFECT WEDDING

Organising your dream nuptials
is one of life's greatest challenges,
whether you're a member of the
Royal Family or not

THE PERFECT HONEYMOON

Like every couple, Prince Harry and Meghan Markle will have wanted their wedding to be perfect. But they'll have been aware that when it comes to the history of royal weddings they are up against some pretty stiff competition. There definitely won't, for instance, have been a present from Mahatma Gandhi, as Harry's grandparents – Queen Elizabeth and the Duke of Edinburgh – received when they got married in 1948. Gandhi's handspun piece of cotton lace, featuring the words "Jai Hind" ("Victory For India") was initially mistaken for a loin cloth. It was just one of the 2,500 gifts the couple were given, which included a racehorse and a Kenyan hunting lodge among several hundred toasters.

Nor will they have had 27 wedding cakes, which is how many Harry's parents – Prince Charles and Lady Diana – had at their wedding in July 1981. But past royal weddings do at least provide a guide for how to plan for the big day, with the royals regularly setting trends when it comes to the key elements – cakes, flowers, dresses and photography. The prevailing theme is a need to reflect the times, but with a touch of class and respect for heritage and tradition.

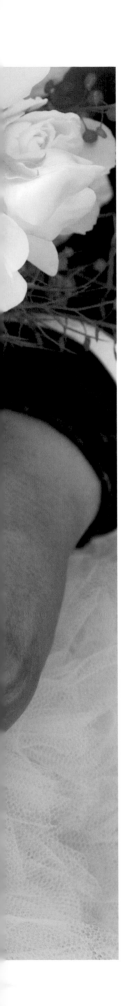

THE PERFECT DRESS

For brides and royal watchers alike, the wedding dress is the most important element. When Elizabeth and Philip got married, it was designed by the favoured royal dressmaker Norman Hartnell and featured national and Commonwealth floral emblems in gold and silver thread. Rationing was ongoing, so the then Princess Elizabeth paid for her dress with clothing coupons. Hartnell was still creating breathtaking designs in 1960, when Princess Margaret's wedding to Antony Armstrong-Jones became the first royal wedding to be broadcast on television. A worldwide audience of 300 million were dazzled by Margaret's dress and Poltimore tiara. A decade later, when Princess Anne married Captain Mark Phillips in 1973, the couple went outside the usual circles and had a simple, medieval-style dress designed by her favourite dressmaker Maureen Baker. By contrast, Sarah Ferguson's dress for her 1986 marriage to Prince Andrew was an embroidered ivory silk gown by Lindka Cierach, featuring the letter "A" for Andrew and Sarah's coat of arms. It had a 17-feet train.

The return to more flamboyant dresses had been started by Princess Diana in 1981, when she wore a wedding dress of breathtakingly puffy extravagance, featuring a 25-foot train of ivory taffeta and antique lace. Designed by David and Elizabeth Emanuel, the dramatic gown featured 10,000 pearls and was said to have cost £9,000. That's a snip compared to Kate Middleton's stunning, stylish long-sleeved dress, which is thought to have cost a six-figure sum. Kate and William's wedding was believed to have come in at around £20 million in total, although a large part of that went on security. If that seems expensive, bear in mind that – when adjusted for inflation – it's reckoned that Charles and Diana's wedding cost around four times as much.

THE PERFECT BOUQUET

Another royal tradition that Meghan continued regards the bouquet, which always contains at least one sprig of myrtle. This dates back to the wedding of Queen Victoria's eldest daughter, Princess Victoria. Myrtle is believed to symbolise hope and love. The decorative flowers for Harry and Meghan's wedding at St George's Chapel were designed by London-based florist Philippa Craddock and consisted of branches of beech, birch and hornbeam, along with white garden roses, peonies and foxgloves.

Myrtle excepted, bouquets have changed over time. Kate Middleton's subtle bouquet by Shane Connolly consisted almost entirely of lily of the valley, while Westminster Abbey was decorated with field maples and hornbeam, at a reputed cost of £50,000. As well as

"
For brides and royal watchers alike, the dress is the most important element"

"

Right: Florist Philippa Craddock, who created the breathtaking floral displays for Harry and Meghan's wedding

being entirely British, these also had symbolic importance – lily of the valley means "trustworthy", hornbeams represent "resilience" and field maples are said stand for "humility and reserve".

By contrast, Princess Diana's bouquet, by Longmans and a gift from the Worshipful Company of Gardeners, was a cascading blend of gardenias, stephanotis, orchids, lily of the valley, roses, freesia, veronica and ivy. Like her dress, it seemed to epitomise the conspicuous opulence of the decade and the jubilation of the occasion. Diana's chosen florist, David Longman, actually made two bouquets in case one was lost, transporting the first by police escort to Buckingham Palace on the morning of the wedding. This was done on the insistence of the Queen, who had lost her own bouquet during the ceremony only to find out it had been thoughtfully placed in an ice box to maintain freshness.

Sarah Ferguson, for her marriage to Prince Andrew, had a small "S"-shaped bouquet by Jane Packer but also wore flowers in her hair – her wedding was so often a case of borrowing ideas from Diana without ever trying to outdo her. As at all royal weddings, the bouquet was later placed on the tomb of the Unknown Soldier in

"

Wedding cakes are so
fun to make and there is
nothing like the wonderful
reactions that you receive
from onlookers

"

THE PERFECT PHOTOGRAPHER

How do you record all this for posterity? The official royal wedding photographer might not be as instantly memorable as the cake, bouquet and dress but it's arguably more important as their photos will be what future historians use to remember the event. Harry and Meghan's chosen photographer was Alexi Lubomirski, a portrait photographer who was born in England to a Peruvian/English mother and Polish/French father. A descendent of Polish royalty, he has photographed stars such as Beyoncé, Gwyneth Paltrow, Natalie Portman, Jennifer Aniston, Jennifer Lopez and Julia Roberts.

While Princess Anne and Mark Philips opted for noted society and fashion photographer Norman Parkinson, Charles and Diana's official photographer was Lord Lichfield, who – as the Queen's first cousin once removed – was able to take more informal images alongside the official portraits. Prince Andrew also chose somebody he knew personally, working closely with Gene Nocon, a Chairman of the Royal Photographic Society and mentor to the Prince, himself a keen amateur photographer. The official portraits were taken by Albert Mackenzie Watson.

Photographers are often resourceful. William and Kate's wedding photos were taken by Hugo Burnand, who managed to get his favourite shot of the couple with bridesmaids and pageboys by bribing the children with sweets, while Sir Geoffrey Shakerley, official photographer for Prince Edward and Sophie Rhys-Jones, had to manipulate some of the images because the then 17-year-old Prince William was looking a bit too sulky.

THE PERFECT MUSIC

Church music tends to be formal, with the wedding march having to be both dignified and optimistic. Diana walked up the aisle as the choir sang "Trumpet Voluntary" by Jeramiah Clarke, while Sarah Ferguson went with Elgar's "Imperial March". Catherine Middleton walked up the aisle to "I Was Glad" by Charles Hubert Hastings Parry, which was composed for the coronation of Edward VII in 1902, while the service itself featured Bach, Britten, Elgar, Vaughan Williams and "Jerusalem" played by the Westminster Abbey Choir, the Chapel Royal Choir, the London Symphony Orchestra and the Central Band of the RAF.

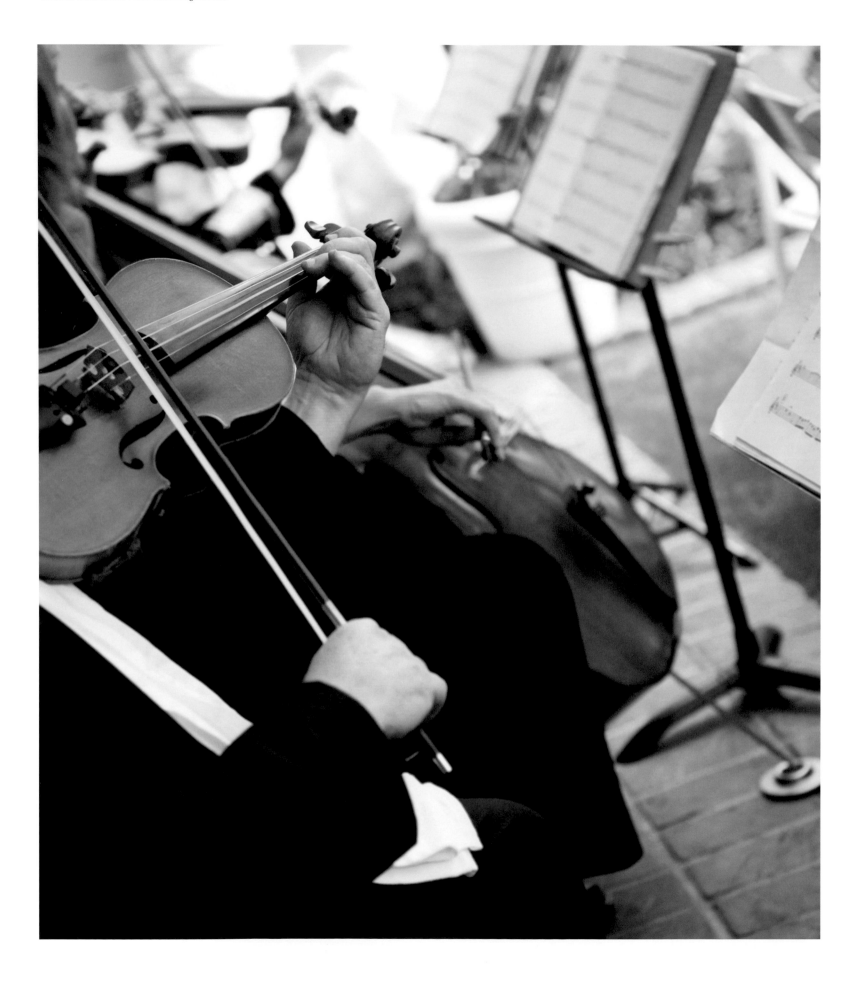

THE PERFECT CATERING

Next comes food. As with everything else, the catering will reflect the spirit of the times, but with a luxurious twist and a focus on British classics. In 1947, Elizabeth and Philip's guests enjoyed Filet de Sole Mountbatten, followed by partridge casserole with salad, green beans and pommes noisette, and an ice-cream bomb ("Bombe Glacee Princesse Elizabeth") for dessert.

Charles and Diana's menu also had a dish named after the bride – Supreme de Volaille Princess de Galles, which was chicken stuffed with lamb mousse – and ended with a very English dish of strawberries and cream. William and Kate used elite caterers Table Talk, who hold a crown listing, which means it is one of the few companies that is permitted to cook and serve food in the Historic Royal Palaces. They served a British menu of hearty but sophisticated dishes, using organic ingredients and on-trend Highgrove spring vegetables.

THE PERFECT DANCE BAND

Following dinner, it's time to take to the dance floor. This usually allows for a more relaxing mix of traditional and contemporary music. At William and Kate's reception, the couple took their first dance to a cover version of Elton John's "Your Song" performed by Ellie Goulding. "I did their first dance and like, talk about scary," Goulding said. "I was so nervous, my hands were shaking." The rest of the evening featured a selection of the usual wedding classics – "She Loves You", "Mr Brightside", a bit of Stevie Wonder, an eyebrow-raising "Sex On Fire" and, of course, "You're The One That I Want".

When Prince Charles and Diana hit the dancefloor in 1981, the music was performed by jazz bandleader Lester Lanin. Lanin was a revered figure in high society – the Queen herself once changed the date of her 60th birthday party just to ensure he could perform. He also played at numerous Presidents' inauguration balls and charged as much as £55,000 a night. People got their money's worth: at Charles and Diana's wedding he played four hours longer than expected, only calling it a day at 3.30am. "That marvellous Lester Lanin," one guest exclaimed, "would have made an earthworm want to dance!"

CULTURED COUTURE

SUZANNE HARWARD

As a young girl growing up in 1960s Australia, Suzanne Harward fell in love with the classic Hollywood musicals of the 1930s and '40s. She remembers sitting wide-eyed in front of her television as a child, in a land of imagination and fantasy, captivated by the couture on her screen.

"I loved to watch Ginger Rogers and Fred Astaire dancing on screen," says Suzanne. "I marvelled at beautiful gowns, wondering how many layers of tulle were in the skirts as they twirled around the dance floor."

It was a love of couture in the old-Hollywood glamour era that inspired her to start designing gowns in 1975. The brand began as a creative partnership with her husband: Suzanne being the creative mind and her husband the business mind. Four decades on, Suzanne Harward is now firmly established as one of Australia's premier couture design houses.

Sourcing luxury textiles directly from European mills, her work features exquisite couture fabrics, intricate hand embellishments and lace appliqué. Suzanne often includes colour in her collections and the now iconic Havana Gown (pictured, opposite) has been embraced by clients worldwide, chosen not only to be worn for weddings, but also as a glamorous gown for prestigious red carpet and gala events.

Suzanne Harward and her team of couturiers' work from an inner-city design studio immersed in a diversely eclectic environment that was once the city's garment district. Drawing her inspiration from beautiful textiles, nature and the world around her, the Suzanne Harward collections offer something for every bride. With a current point of view, she merges trend-driven concepts with a keen understanding of her diverse clientele. Details like chic cut-outs, textural fabrications, 3D appliqués and micro-pleating give the collections a modern feel that is fresh, fashion-forward and sophisticated. Each gown is expertly hand-made in the Melbourne atelier under the direction of Suzanne herself.

A self-taught prodigy, Suzanne's design process is organic and intuitive. She begins by choosing a beautiful fabric then draping on the form as the fabric speaks to her. "It truly is a magical experience," says her daughter Brooke, who works alongside her mother in the family business. "True couture is a vanishing art and, in a world of fast fashion, it is becoming increasingly difficult to find garments that are made with the level of care and expertise that we offer. We are incredibly proud that we are keeping the traditional art of couture alive."

As well as designing bespoke couture gowns for women in Australia, a strong presence on social media has played a pivotal role in launching Suzanne Harward as an international brand. The label is now carried by boutiques in the US and the UK and receives daily enquiries from across the globe, with more and more consultations now taking place on Skype.

The joy of working one-on-one with each bride is what continues to propel the business forward. "Dressing a bride is such a privilege," says Suzanne. "Our couture stylists travel the journey with her and it is always a wonderful moment to see each bride's happiness at finding the dress that truly expresses who she is. We want each bride to feel as though she's the most beautiful version of herself. We get to experience a bride's perfect moment, it is the most beautiful dress she will ever wear."

Such a significant event of the Royal Wedding between Prince Harry and Meghan Markle reignites the majestic grandeur of couture. "The dream lives on," says Suzanne, "the dream of keeping couture alive."

www.suzanneharward.com

CHEESE DREAMS

VROMAGE

"I always said that if it doesn't taste good, no one will give up cheese," says Youssef Vromage, the founder of Los Angeles-based shop Vromage. Opened in August 2014 on that city's famous Sunset Boulevard, Vromage sells artisan cheese, but with one big difference – it's entirely vegan. Youssef, however, wasn't. In fact, the 63-year-old of Lebanese descent, raised in Casablanca and Paris, used to be a restaurateur in Santa Barbara and used to eat meat – until, in 2009, after moving to LA, he met a woman who changed all that.

"I was chasing this beautiful woman who was a vegan," he explains, "so I decided I was going to be vegetarian so I could hang out with her, hoping for romance. One day, she put nuts in the blender and tried to make this vegan cheese – and it did not taste good! I wanted to impress her. 'That's not cheese!' I said. 'I'll show you how to make cheese!'"

Youssef then spent years developing his creation, making it from nut milk and giving his friends samples as he attempted to perfect it and woo the woman in question. Incredibly, his efforts paid off. "I started making all these cheeses hoping that one day we would have this romantic relationship," he laughs. "It took a while, but in that while I made so many cheeses and everybody thought I was crazy. But everybody who tried it said how good it tasted."

The relationship didn't last, but Fakhouri's vision did. After many years of making his vegan cheese and testing it out on those close to him, he eventually opened his shop. Less than three years later, he makes between 17 to 20 varieties of artisanal (but vegan) cheese that many claim is better than the actual thing. In fact, Fakhouri has tricked professional chefs into thinking they were eating real cheese. He uses only the finest ingredients – imported fresh truffles and organic nuts from Europe – and makes everything himself. He has even changed his surname by deed-poll to Fakhouri to Vromage. "This is a true artisan, dairy-free cheese," he says. "There's no recipe written down. I come in and I make the cheeses and it requires a lot of tasting. Italians use it in pasta and pizza because they think it tastes better than using real cheese."

Youssef puts the secret of his success down to one thing – he's not trying to replicate the taste of dairy-based cheese, but make a "new food". Although Vromage is 100 per cent vegan, it is not marketed to vegans – Youssef wants it to be for everybody, but especially those with allergies who thought they were condemned to a life without dairy.

"I get overwhelmed when I see how excited they get," he says, "because some of them thought they'd never have cheese again. They get very emotional. Most of my customers aren't vegan – they're just regular people."

That, though, is not strictly true. Vromage has started picking up a number of regular high-profile customers and fans, including Ellen DeGeneres, Alicia Silverstone, James Cameron, Danny DeVito, Beau Bridges, Kathryn Bigelow and Moby. And while he's keen for the whole world to experience the taste of Vromage, Youssef is also emphatic about it remaining an artisan product that succeeds primarily because of how it tastes rather than what it is. After all, it was born out of true love and passion, and he believes it should stay that way. Or, as Youssef Vromage himself puts it: "People don't come because it's vegan – they come become it's really good!"
www.vromage.com

MY KIND OF GOWN

JUSTIN ALEXANDER

Launched in Brooklyn just after the Second World War as a mom-and-pop bridal accessories business, Justin Alexander now rules supreme: six wedding dress brands, from high-end to commercial, renowned across the wedding world. Now in its third generation, the family-owned business has become a market leader. It is stocked in 250 stores in the UK and Ireland and has won 10 UK bridal awards in the past 15 years. As well as the commercial successes of its Lillian West, Sincerity Bridal, and Sweetheart ranges, the brand also boasts award-winning luxury labels, and collaborations with leading couturiers such as Viktor&Rolf Mariage.

Justin Alexander Warshaw, Creative Director and President, recently returned from the *Elle* International Bridal Awards 2018, where the brand's work on Viktor&Rolf Mariage's Fall-Winter Collection helped win Best Bridal Gown Collection. Judges declared each design in the collection "unique... like a piece of art".

But Warshaw never rests on his laurels. Just a few days after the win, he launched the campaign for Justin Alexander Signature's new collection, shot on location on the black volcanic sands of Lanzarote.

"We always like to shoot with a juxtaposition," Warshaw explains. "This time the outdoor space of Lanzarote was the perfect destination because of its great beauty. It's so unusual."

"Lanzarote is such a stark and moody setting," adds Mandy Hjellming Chua, Justin Alexander's Marketing Director. "We were able to take advantage of the location and its dramatic lighting to add a nice contrast to a very glamorous style. As Justin said, it's very unexpected."

The new Signature collection follows hot on the heels of Justin Alexander's "Be You" campaign, in which influential model and body-positivity champion Iskra Lawrence donned designs in chantilly lace, organza lace and silk dupion, with rich beading. The shoot was a chance to highlight the brand's longstanding approach to body-positive styling. Justin Alexander dresses run from a UK size 4 upwards, and the brand does not charge extra for plus-size gowns. For years several of the Justin Alexander collections have offered style modifications with better support for higher sizes, and the brand has recently introduced plus-size samples for trunk shows so every customer can see herself represented.

"We're really focused on inclusive sizing and making dresses that work with all body types," says Warshaw. "We're very conscious that, although the trend might be plunging backs and plunging fronts, a single style doesn't work for everybody."

"We want to give the best experience to every bride, regardless of her shape, size, style, and personality," says Chua. "We see the house of Justin Alexander as the solution for all brides." Chua notes that the response to the Iskra Lawrence campaign has been "incredible". "Just looking through the comments on Instagram for instance we've had a lot of brides come and say, 'Wow, I've been nervous about shopping until now', or 'I never thought a style like this would be flattering on my body,' or, 'Thank you, you've given me the inspiration and confidence I needed'."

After the success of the Viktor&Rolf collaboration, Warshaw has another link-up in his sights. This autumn, the brand will pair up with a big-name British designer who has previously worked with London fashion giants, the late Alexander McQueen, and Matthew Williamson. Brides looking for inspiration and confidence before next year's wedding season couldn't do better than to look to Justin Alexander. *www.justinalexander.com*

THE IMMACULATE RECEPTION

WILDFLOWER LINEN

From exquisite table linen and chair covers to stylish napkins and placemats, brides and bridegrooms want everything to look absolutely perfect on their wedding day. With that in mind, many happy couples turn to Youngsong Martin, a fashion designer who launched Wildflower Linen in 2001.

Martin got the idea for her business after helping her niece to plan her wedding reception and discovering a scarcity of beautiful linens to decorate the wedding tables and chairs. "In fashion, one goes to a lot of events," she says. "Although textiles are very important to that industry, it seemed that so much more could be done with the most important and abundant elements in the room – tables and chairs. So I literally brought all my ideas to the proverbial table and I haven't looked back."

She named the company Wildflower Linen after asking herself: "What is beautiful and unexpected, yet dependable? Wildflowers in bloom seemed to suit my vision." Seventeen years later, Wildflower Linen is a leading designer and producer of table linens, chair covers and table accessories for weddings, banquets and prestigious events around the world, both for rent and hire. Her clients range from brides to event planners to famous designers and celebrities.

She provides materials in a dazzling range of colours, designing everything herself – from hand-beaded linens embroidered with sequins and pearls to elegant white lace. Accessories include decorative napkins, napkin rings and bands, placemats, and throw pillows. Nature and history are a huge inspiration to her, although the location of an event often influences her too.

Based in Buena Park, California, Wildflower Linen has a range of showrooms in the US, including Beverly Hills, Napa Valley, San Francisco, Dallas and Maui. It is often associated with high-profile events and Martin's creations have been the pièce de résistance at glittering events held by Oprah Winfrey and Elton John, the post-Oscars Governors Ball, *Vanity Fair* magazine's after-parties and a White House luncheon for the First Lady of France. Wildflower Linen designs are even featured in Edward and Bella's wedding scene in *The Twilight Saga: Breaking Dawn*.

The team don't just deal with high-end occasions, though, but with events of all sizes and budgets. The custom-designed chair covers and romantic, classic styles are particularly sought after.

"The company prides itself on creating designs to fulfil every want, whim or fancy," says Martin. "We can also make beautiful custom-made prints to order. I work closely with clients to bring their ideas to fruition. Primarily I act as an editor to shape my clients' personal visions. Wildflower's inventory affords me a virtually limitless palette of colour, texture and style options. Romance and subtlety are the prevailing trends of the moment. White, ivory and gold are hot this year."

When she advises couples about their wedding tables, she always takes their own individual styles into account. "A design needs to be cohesive, so some restraint must be expressed," she says. "Yet the bride and groom must have their own personal styles expressed and interpreted to make an unforgettable statement on their special day."

Martin often draws on her experience as a fashion designer. "I'm still a fashion designer, you might say. Now, however, it's the entire room that wears my designs – especially the chairs and tables."
www.wildflowerlinens.com

TIME FOR TEA

NEWBY TEAS

Tea may now be the most popular beverage on the planet, but for centuries it was reserved for only the wealthiest in Western society. However, it remains a luxury for drinkers of Newby Teas. Established just 18 years ago by philanthropist, businessman and tea-devotee Nirmal Sethia, Newby's success is largely down to its commitment to quality. Sethia's interest and extensive knowledge about tea stems from his years of training as an apprentice tea taster at Plantation House in London and in the tea gardens of Assam. It was his unparalleled passion for the art of tea that drove him to establish Newby in 2000.

"We're not based on false marketing or promoting something that the product is not," explains Aneta Aslakhanova, the company's Global Marketing Director. "We pay a lot of attention to design and packaging, so everything is up to a luxury standard. But the quality of the tea is the main priority and that's something we never compromise on."

The company's unique advantage is its state-of-the-art packaging facility based just outside Kolkata. Built to ensure freshness, the unique factory holds temperature and humidity controlled chambers for green, black and flavoured tea leaves, and ensures that the blends can be packed as close as possible to where they are grown, guaranteeing supreme and unparalleled freshness in every variety.

"It is not good practice for tea leaves to be transported all the way from east to west and then be stored and packed in the warehouses across Europe," says Aslakhanova. "Tea is a fragile product, so if you're buying the best there's no point bringing it here and destroying the quality of it in the process."

Sethia's dedication to quality standards has paid off, with Newby winning a slew of awards. Most prized of all are the accolades from the Global Tea Championship – an independent competition judged by international tea professionals.

Newby's focus on quality has been key to building the brand's reputation among business and consumer clients worldwide. The house made its name in the hospitality sector, stocking teas for luxury hotels including Gleneagles in Scotland and the Burj Al Arab in Dubai, as well as several Michelin-starred restaurants. In 2015, Newby appeared on Waitrose shelves, and in 2017 was added to select branches of Sainsbury's.

But investment has not focused solely on the product. Sethia's philanthropic pursuits founded the non-profit, UK-registered charity, the N Sethia Foundation, which supports unique projects in education, medicine and social welfare around the world. The foundation also owns the Chitra Collection, the world's largest and finest private collection of historic teawares. The collection was founded in memory of Nirmal's late wife Chitra and comprises more than 1,700 pieces, including tea caddies by Fabergé, a teapot owned by Admiral Lord Nelson, Winston Churchill's daughter's teapot, President Roosevelt's tea caddy and a tea set belonging to Napoleon Bonaparte's right-hand man.

Newby Teas takes pride in launching limited editions for special events. Its tea-themed advent calendars sell out annually, and themed caddies are a highlight of each Chinese New Year. This summer, Newby celebrates the royal wedding with six of its best-selling blends from their luxury Silken Pyramid range, presented in limited-edition packaging, inspired by the Lover's Knot tiara that was a favourite of Diana, Princess of Wales.

"For so many years, tea was a luxury that wasn't affordable to everyone," says Aslakhanova. "There's such a huge amount of history in tea: so much love, art and craft has gone into creating teawares. That's where a lot of our inspiration comes from." Now more accessible than ever, tea's heritage lives on at Newby.
www.newbyteas.co.uk

A GLASS ACT

VERA PURE

We don't know how Harry and Meghan will toast their nuptials, but an elegant choice would be with these iridescent champagne flutes created for the Royal Wedding by Swiss designer Vera Purtscher and her design studio Vera Pure. The perfect marriage of classical and contemporary styles, they feature engraved initials by a glass master and a sculptural base cut from a block of flawless glass.

"My wedding two years ago was the most wonderful day of my life and I wish Meghan and Harry the same joy," says Purtscher of her decision to create a unique gift for the couple. "Harry and Meghan are lovely people and Meghan, as a former food blogger, shares the passion for food and classy fine dining table arrangements!"

Creating beautiful things for the dining table has been Purtscher's passion for more than three decades. Her aim is to create functional pieces with a poetic touch. Sustainability and timelessness are in the core of her design philosophy. This reflects in her very first design collection, the MoonLashes silverware, a handcrafted and ergonomic industrial design series. To optimise the eating experience, Vera Pure even offers left- and right-handed cutlery.

The distinctive SinStella range of glassware, from which she took Harry and Meghan's gift, was launched last year. It started as a pragmatic way to solve the problem of delicate-stemmed wine glasses breaking easily. By separating the foot from the stem and the bowl, Purtscher showed her bold architectural approach. Just as a sculptor cuts his masterpiece out of a marble stone, the SinStella base is cut out of some of the world's most precious, flawless optical glass. This little sculpture holds the most beautiful crystal glass inputs, from a champagne flute to a floating plate, adding to the feeling of exclusivity and elegance on the table.

Purtscher originally trained as architect in Vienna, before turning her gaze to table wear and launching her studio Vera Pure in 1997. "The rules of architecture still apply to what I do," she says. "You need to consider proportion, materials, cost, the effect of light on the surfaces and so on. My silverware, porcelain and glasses are tools, but they are also little nomadic pieces of architecture."

Vera Pure does not just equip royal families, but some of the world's top gastronomic destinations, including Marcus Wareing's Michelin-starred restaurant at The Berkeley Hotel in London, Heinz Reitbauer's Steirereck in Vienna (ranked 10th in the World's 50 Best Restaurants) and the eponymous Manhattan restaurant of the former MoMA chef Gabriel Kreuther, where the SinStella glasses were awarded "the best dish of the year 2017" by the New York Post.

Inspired by the Japanese "Wabi-Sabi" philosophy and the Italian design esprit, Vera Pure's innovative yet enduring tableware creations are a nod to culinary art. With a passion for sustainability and a mission to elevate the fine dining experience, these pieces have an admirable artisanal value.

A few years ago, Vera Purtscher's son Johannes joined the family business he grew up with to further build on the brand and make the outstanding designs even better known. "Our design studio stands for highest exclusivity and innovativeness realized in delicate handicraft," he says. "My aim is to increase the visibility and availability of Vera Pure inventions."

Vera Pure's story is all about love: from Purtscher's first encounter with design through to her aesthetic, her drive and her relationships. And this is reflected in her products. Timeless designs that will last for ever: it's hard to think of a more perfect way to toast a wedding. Cheers! *www.verapu.re*

THE PERFECT TONIC

NB GIN

When two lawyers decided to make their own artisan gin in 2011 they never dreamed it would become an award-winning brand with customers all over the world.

Husband and wife Steve and Vivienne Muir started NB Gin in the kitchen of their home in the seaside town of North Berwick on the east coast of Scotland. The couple had no knowledge of the drinks industry, but using a pressure cooker, a thermometer and old central heating pipes they spent thousands of hours creating "the perfect gin".

"Our kitchen became an official ginnery," says CEO Vivienne Muir. "Through trial and error, we worked out the perfect blend of botanicals, using a mix of juniper, coriander seed, angelica root, grains of paradise, lemon peel, cassia bark, cardamom and orris root. We launched our gin in 2013 and we suddenly started getting orders for thousands of bottles. A lot of my family live in North Berwick and they helped us to hand-fill the bottles using glass jugs."

NB Gin – named after North Berwick and the phrase *nota bene* (Latin for "note well") – grew steadily. After investing in a custom-built still, the Muirs started exporting to Germany and Spain, and in 2015 their Original NB Gin was voted the World's Best London Dry Gin. Their NB Navy Strength Gin (57 per cent proof) won gold medals at the Global Gin Masters and the Scottish Gin Awards in 2017.

More accolades followed. Johnny Roxburgh, the celebrated "party architect", was so impressed that he started serving it at his parties. NB Gin was also selected to be served at the Sony Brit Awards after-party.

NB Gin now sells four products – NB Gin, NB Navy, NB Vodka and NB Tonic. NB Rum ("a full-bodied golden rum") will launch later in 2018. The company has also signed a deal to sell its drinks in at least nine states across the USA. "We've gone from delivering bottles in small boxes to preparing a 40 ft shipping container," says Muir. The company recently opened a new distillery and visitors' centre, offering luxury distillery tours, giving visitors the chance to learn how the premium spirits are produced, ending with a tasting.

The Muirs are very proud of NB Gin and say it is the perfect celebratory drink. "Gin has had a real renaissance and we were one of the first craft gins in the UK," says Muir, whose favourite drink is NB Gin with ice, a light tonic like NB tonic water and a blood orange with some lemon thyme. "Our brand is sophisticated, clean and very special."

www.nbdistillery.com

THE PERFECT HONEYMOON

HIMALAYAN HEDONISM

EASTERN SAFARIS

If we've heard of the Himalayan mountain kingdom of Bhutan at all, we know it for its remoteness and its historical isolation from tourism and westernisation – and also for being the only country in the world that measures success not by Gross Domestic Product but by Gross National Happiness. For Eastern Safaris owners Brett Melzer and Khin Omar Win, Bhutan is also home to their luxury retreat Gangtey Lodge, the ultimate fulfilment of their desire to establish a sustainable luxury escape. Opened in November 2013, Gangtey Lodge was voted the fifth best hotel in Asia by readers of *Condé Nast Traveler* in 2017.

Win and Melzer first met in Myanmar in 1997 and were engaged within months of meeting. At the time Win worked in development and she shared with Melzer a frustration over the slow progress that charities and NGOs faced in the field, while businesses enjoyed a lot more freedom. So together they developed the concept behind Eastern Safaris. "We wanted to create products and amazing experiences based on our belief that travel should have meaning," says Win, "and that our journeys should have a positive impact on the places that we visit."

"We really wanted to create something adventurous and innovative," says Melzer. "Any business has to be commercial, but we wanted to focus on balancing that with development and sustainability."

Political upheaval forced the closure of their first hotel in the far north of Myanmar after two years – though their iconic hot air ballooning company "Balloons over Bagan" continues to thrive. In 2004 the couple visited Bhutan to look for a suitable spot for a new venture. After several visits they eventually discovered a site in the beautiful Gangtey Valley, best known for its native black-necked cranes and a 17th-century university for Buddhist monks.

"Gangtey Valley is a pristine nature reserve," says Win. "It was a place of total authenticity and we wanted to enable our guests to connect and immerse themselves in the culture and the spirituality of this beautiful country."

Win and Melzer built the 12-room luxury lodge to blend in harmoniously with its surroundings, with no signage and in the style of a traditional farmhouse. The 54 Bhutanese staff are all local to the area, recruited, trained and promoted in-house. The lodge is warmed by underfloor heating and every en suite room has a cosy fireplace and spectacular mountain views. The dining room serves locally sourced, seasonal and organic Bhutanese food and international dishes. A traditional hot stone bathhouse adds a touch of rustic elegance and indulgence, and is a popular way to soak and relax in at the end of the day.

The lodge organises full and half-day excursions and activities, some in association with the local community, from visits to the monastery and local temples, farms and villages to hiking and mountain biking through the pine forests. Guests can also learn the traditional Bhutanese sport of archery, a national obsession – village archery contests are fiercely contested by men and women around the country.

Win and Melzer have grown to love their adopted community, celebrating last Christmas at the lodge with the family (for their children, the highlight of the season was harvesting turnips and making yak butter at a local farmhouse). Yaks aside, what the pair love most about their luxury retreat is the place itself: the green patchwork of fields on the valley floor, mist on the mountains and sunshine breaking through the clouds in the cool, quiet mornings at 10,000 feet. Bhutan's Gross National Happiness is on the rise.

www.gangteylodge.com

ISLAND LUXURY

THE MULIA, MULIA RESORT & VILLAS, NUSA DUA, BALI

With clear views across the Indian Ocean, the photogenic images taken by guests at any one of the Mulia establishments in Bali are now a common sight on many social media accounts. Mulia Resort holds a prime spot on the beach in Nusa Dua – a long stretch of white sand on Bali's southern peninsula, Bukit. The Mulia is insistently luxurious: it's a suite-only establishment, and guests can ensure total relaxation thanks to ocean or garden views, an in-house butler service and each suite's individual outdoor Jacuzzi.

Besides The Mulia, Mulia Villas also offers guests a resort and villas to choose from. Its 108 villas were designed with privacy in mind: each one has its own private hydrotherapy pool, day bed and terrace, as well as beautiful views of the gardens. And they're not just for couples, either. As well as the one-bed villas, there are also multi-room villas including the two-storey, three-bed Presidential Villa and the six-bed Mulia Mansion.

When it first opened five years ago, Mulia Bali was named one of the world's most romantic hotels in the 2013 *Conde Nast Traveler* Hot List. It was among the magazine's best resorts in 2016 and last year ranked among CNT's Readers' Choice destinations in Asia, with celebrated features including its excellent service, great food and good atmosphere.

Last summer, Mulia Bali extended its complex even further by adding a 2,000 sq m exclusive beachfront event venue with enough space for weddings and conferences of up to 1,000 people. "The Unity Garden was launched to accommodate the demand for beachfront events and weddings," says a spokesperson. "Located at the end of Nusa Dua bay, it provides a secluded and exclusive venue that is perfect for wedding receptions and grand events, overlooking the white-sand beach all the way to the Indian Ocean on the horizon as well as the Balinese Geger Temple perched on the cliff." Weddings at Mulia Bali are personalised, thanks to its designated wedding consultants and choice of venues. Distinctive venues cater for services, from intimate nuptials and blessings, to large-scale flamboyant wedding celebrations.

Guests at Mulia Bali can make use of the four restaurants and five bars in the wider Mulia complex, as well as the spa, fitness centre and tennis courts. The hotel also boasts six pools, the most scenic of which is the Oasis: a beachside spot where guests can watch waves rolling in at a cool remove. Whatever the holiday, Mulia Bali's menu of resort packages helps guests create a holiday shaped around the individual's unique approach to unwinding.

The Mulia revels in its setting. The towering statues of Balinese women that line the beachfront pool have become an icon of luxury travel in Bali. Mulia Bali dining destinations feature various cuisines from around the world while keeping authentic local touches. Mulia Spa capitalises on Bali's rich heritage as a spice-trading island and, beyond the 75-acre complex, the concierge has a world of suggestions for exploring southern Bali's temples, cities and coasts. The nearby golf club awaits those with a passion for the game, but the likelihood is that you'll find all the rest and relaxation you're looking for on the doorstep of your accommodation. How you choose to spend your time is your luxury.
www.themulia.com

FIT FOR A FAIRY TALE

TOUCAN HILL

"Magic, fantasy and romance." Those are the words that guests use about Toucan Hill. It's the most fanciful, improbable villa on one of the world's most fanciful, unbelievable islands. Toucan Hill is a luxurious Moorish structure perched high above the tropical greenery of Mustique; a Caribbean island as intimate and exclusive as it is beautiful and romantic.

Tatiana and Gerret Copeland first experienced Mustique in the days when Lord Glenconner, who bought the island in 1958, revived and transformed it into a destination for the rich and glamorous. Lord Glenconner regularly hosted close friend Princess Margaret at his famous costume parties in Mustique.

Tatiana Copeland drew inspiration from her travels and came up with a magical palace whose style lays somewhere between Morocco and the Alhambra. Its richly planted grounds and white, sugar-sand beaches complete the setting.

"That view remains a jaw-dropper," says Copeland, the businesswoman and philanthropist who spent ten years creating the house. "I wanted to create a wow factor when you first come in. Guests really do walk in and say 'WOW' out loud. I wanted it to be completely different from what rational people have in their lives. It's a house you would never live in, in your real life. This is a fun, fantasy house. People who rent the villa step away from reality."

Toucan Hill offers privacy, serenity and romance, and is available for celebrations such as honeymoons and family gatherings or simply to enjoy an indulgent, secluded stay in paradise. "Being here is an extraordinary, beautiful experience," says Copeland, "even in the life of the most jaded traveller."

It's like the *1,001 Nights* tales – and then some. The details are endless. There are dazzling mother-of-pearl inlaid tables, silver furniture, art work with precious gems, Moroccan arches and tiles, mosaic fountains, and a domed dining pavilion. Outside, bougainvillea and hibiscus add splashes of bright colour against the cool white walls. By day, sunshine floods the terraces and the turquoise infinity pool; by night, the glow of lanterns and the scent of jasmine predominate.

Toucan Hill includes four luxury suites with their own balconies, a master pavilion, two private infinity pools, the use of two vehicles and a staff of seven. It takes full advantage of the spectacular views and breezes that cool the hilltop estate, which is available to rent through the Mustique Company.

The attentive full-time staff (estate manager, butler, chef, two housekeepers, houseman and gardener) are on hand to organise dinners, beach picnics, parties, spa treatments and water sports sessions – however much or little the guests choose to do. The chef at Toucan Hill will prepare delicious meals made with locally grown produce and the freshest seafood. "Our staff provides an incredible service," says Copeland. "It's not just a building and a gorgeous fantasy. I'm blessed with a fabulous manager and a discreet and professional butler. They know when to leave guests in peace and when to help. They are there to see to all guests' daily needs. They make the house come alive."

Luxury travel defined by a spirit of adventure, enchantment, fantasy, passion and excitement can all begin with your unique stay at Toucan Hill. "Even if you are used to luxury travel, there is a special atmosphere in the house – a spirit of romance and fantasy – that really is unique."
www.toucanhill.com

KIWIS BIG ADVENTURE

AROHA LUXURY NEW ZEALAND TOURS

New Zealand is often described as one of the most romantic places on earth. Tranquil and breathtakingly beautiful, it's the ultimate escape for many couples. It's no wonder, then, that Harry and Meghan were rumoured to be considering it as a destination for their honeymoon.

"New Zealand has become a real draw for honeymooners," says Veronika Vermeulen, owner of the concierge travel company Aroha Luxury New Zealand Tours. "From fabulous private lodges to extraordinary gastronomy to unique adventures, you'll find everything here that you could possibly want from a luxurious break with your partner."

No one knows more about New Zealand's finer experiences than Vermeulen. Her company specialises in tailor-made tours, hosted by a personal driver-guide. "No two of our holidays are the same," she says. "We start from scratch with each client and we work with a wide range of providers to give guests the chance to have exclusive experiences and to get to know New Zealand in a very personal way."

Vermeulen's guides have helicoptered travellers on to active volcanoes and arranged for them to take private jetboats along the river from the sea to the mountain. "Nothing is out of our league," she says. "If you want to enjoy a gourmet meal on top of a glacier, we can do it for you. Our guides will go out of their way to help with any request."

For Vermeulen, the magic of New Zealand is its diversity. "Every landscape you can think of is here," she says. "It's possible to ski in the morning and then surf in the afternoon. Over a two-week trip, you could see fjords, mountains, deserts, rainforests and glaciers."

Vermeulen, originally from Berlin, first came to New Zealand 20 years ago. "I was instantly struck with its warmth and beauty. I moved here without a job or any connections, but I've never regretted it. New Zealand is the most extraordinary playground on earth."

Her team of experts includes a former member of the New Zealand Symphony Orchestra, a ski instructor and a TV production coordinator. "Our guides are very cultured people, with excellent people skills," she says. "They're not extroverts. They know when holidaymakers want time on their own."

The focus is always on creating an unforgettable trip of a lifetime. "We do this because we want to share our passion for New Zealand," she says. "We hope people will come here and fall in love."

www.arohatours.co.nz

Chapter Thirteen

ETERNAL ELEGANCE

"Doubt thou the stars are
Doubt the sun doth
Doubt truth be a li
but never doub
I love.

—Willia

JEWELLERY FIT FOR A PRINCESS

NADRI

In 1840, the day before Queen Victoria's wedding, Prince Albert presented his bride-to-be with a huge sapphire brooch encircled by 12 round diamonds. A generation later, Victoria's daughter-in-law, Queen Alexandra of Denmark, wore a tiara gifted to her by her future husband Edward VII to wear on her wedding day. The tiara was dripping with diamonds, intended as a striking display of Edward's love. For the reigning monarch, the choice was a token of affection from her mother who lent Elizabeth a tiara made up of 47 diamond bars. Disaster was narrowly avoided when, two hours before the ceremony, the tiara snapped and was rushed to a royal jeweller to be mended at speed.

The British monarchy throughout history have expressed their love with precious metal and exquisite stones that have been handed down from generation to generation for each royal bride to wear.

Today, across the Atlantic in 2018, jeweller Nadri is showing its own admiration for the newest royal couple, Prince Harry and Meghan Markle. Inspired by the royals' engagement, and what is known about the wedding ceremony and their honeymoon, Nadri created the Nova Bridal Collection, imagining what the couple would wear and what would suit this modern pair.

"We looked at the Royal Family and their traditions: the sapphire stone and the important role it's played in jewellery throughout Great Britain's history," says Nadri founder Young Tae MacGyver Choi.

For instance, the deep-blue-coloured stone in Nadri's collection pays homage to Prince Harry's late mother, Diana, Princess of Wales. In 1981, Prince Charles let Diana choose her own ring. She picked a Ceylon sapphire stone surrounded by diamonds and set in white gold. When Diana died, the ring reportedly went to Prince Harry while Prince William inherited a Cartier watch. However, it's suspected that the brothers made a pact – and whoever married first would give the ring to his fiancée. The ring chosen by the Princess of Wales, and which Kate Middleton, the Duchess of Cambridge, now wears is a design that can also be traced back to another royal jewel, the sapphire brooch given to Queen Victoria.

The combination of sapphire and diamonds of old inspired Nadri to create the Nova collection designed around what a young bride would wear to the celebrations surrounding the wedding. A sterling silver sunburst mimics the shape of a crown to become a tiara necklace, a bracelet, earrings and cluster brooch.

"The sunburst and star motifs are suggestive of Great Britain's royal emblems, combined with the symbolism we associate with the United States," says Choi. "For the wedding day, we imagined a tapered collar necklace made of hundreds of cubic zirconia stones set in sterling silver. As with the Nova collection, all settings are hand-linked, creating a fluid and flexible piece fit for a modern royal. The coordinating chandelier earrings and hair comb make for graceful, contemporary bridal jewellery."

It's that modernity that has drawn Nadri, specialists in classic-yet-fashionable jewellery, to the couple. Prince Harry and Meghan are ushering in a new era for the royals, cooler and more relaxed than ever before. Their gentle disruption of protocol was captured in their engagement photographs shot by Alexi Lubomirski, which would not have looked out of place in a glossy magazine. Lubomirski's photography seemed to capture the couple's genuine love for each other and the pictures inspired Nadri.

"Our engagement ring's centre-stone represents Harry and Meghan's love and life together," says Choi. "The horizontal 1.5-carat marquise diamond is anchored with two smaller round diamonds and surrounded by hand-engraved pavé bands. The design symbolises individuals that come together to make something bigger." To mark the final celebrations, the honeymoon is commemorated with the Eclipse collection made of 14-karat gold and diamonds.

But these collections are not just in honour of Harry and Meghan. They're for all modern brides and Nadri's loyal following of customers. Thousands have been attracted to the brand by their appreciation of fine jewellery.

Choi knows only too well what it is to want sparkle in your life. Growing up in the South Korean town of Goseong-gun, the son of a poor farmer who milled rice for his village, he had never even seen jewellery until he went on a school trip to a history museum in Korea. "I saw jewellery for the first time in my life at the history museum," he says. "It captivated me in a mysterious way."

The jewellery that fascinated him adorned another royal family – the Silla dynasty who ruled one of the three ancient kingdoms of Korea from 57 BC. Seeing the beautiful and delicate work, Choi decided he couldn't follow in his father's footsteps – he had to create jewellery instead. That moment changed the course of his life.

Choi founded Nadri in 1984 and moved across the world to New York where he took the company international. But before that jewellery led Choi to his wife. "I met her when we both worked in the jewellery industry in Korea," he says.

Can he offer any expert advice to Prince Harry and Meghan? "I feel that in any relationship it is important to respect each other's style," he says. "May they always acknowledge and love each other's true inner self. We wish the couple well as they embark upon a life filled with happiness and service."
www.nadri.com

NATURAL BEAUTY

CAROLYN LO

Carolyn Lo loves colour. It was all the beautiful variations of colours and shades that first attracted her to fine natural gemstones and led her to design glamorous jewellery. "I use different shapes, shades and whatever I can bring out of the stone," she says.

Without formal training, Lo began by working for Liebermann Waelchli, agents for Cartier and Chanel with a 100-year history of trading Asian and European luxury goods. Her desire to design eventually took over and Lo struck out on her own.

"I was always attracted to gemstones but I couldn't find the right jeweller to mount the stone in the style I wanted," says Lo. "So I started to design my own jewellery." Her leap of faith paid off. "Friends liked my designs and asked me to make jewellery for them. They referred me to their friends and I continued to get more and more commissions." Lo's store in Taiwan recently celebrated its fifth anniversary and she now has clients across the world – with her sights next set on London.

Lo's designs are all one-off pieces, either starting from scratch or redesigning or transforming an inherited piece of jewellery. "It's about the character you can bring out of the stones," she says. "I just see a gemstone which I like and have a feel for. I then design for that stone and decide on the style."

This style is naturally influenced by Lo's inspirations. "I enjoy architecture, interior design and paintings such as Claude Monet's Water Lilies series," she says. "I like the way Monet paints, layer upon layer. I want to do that with my jewellery. I am inspired by colour combinations. I also like my designs to have different angles. Nothing flat. I prefer 3-D."

Lo achieves this layering effect by cleverly combining a variety of materials. "I usually use two or three colours of gold per piece," she says. "It doesn't have to be white gold. I use black gold, oxidised gold, rose gold and yellow gold. I just put everything together and see how it goes." Lo's Taiwanese heritage plays a part in her designs too, particularly in her use of fine jade. "I don't just use green jade," she clarifies. "There is also white, purple, and even different shades of green jade – some blue, some yellow. But my designs aren't just about traditional Chinese culture. For design you have to have a free mind."

Decorations, often of natural subjects, provide the final flourish. "I like my jewellery to have movement. So, most of the time, you can move around the small flower, butterfly, bee or starfish which I have attached to the main stone." Lo's style is glamorous and fun, a good example being her beautiful jadeite and sapphire maple-leaf brooch, enhanced by black gold with a ladybird dangling off the side.

But in the end, says Lo, there is more to a piece of jewellery than just the design. "The first time I touched some antique Victorian jewellery, I could feel the creator's passion. That's why my work is all made by hand. Hopefully my pieces will give people that same feeling a long time from now. One customer told me that she feels more beautiful once she puts on my jewellery. For some people, food is comfort but, for me, a nice piece of jewellery is comfort. You look at the colour, you put on your ring, you look at the mirror and think, 'Wow, I look fantastic.' And, of course, that cheers you up, right?"
www.carolynlo.com

STONE LOVE

KOHINOOR JEWELLERS

Agra is a city steeped in history, famous for the iconic white marble Taj Mahal, built by Mughal emperor Shah Jahan. The former Mughal capital has for centuries also been home to jewellers, artisans and artists inspired by the rich heritage around them.

Family-owned and now in its fifth generation, the exclusive, appointment-only Kohinoor Jewellers creates distinctive pieces for a discerning global clientele. "Our business developed out of our heritage," says owner Ghanshyam Mathur. "Now we work with a contemporary fusion of art and jewellery based on Indian art, architecture and paintings."

The Mathur family's ancestors came to the old walled city of Agra in 1857 with the court of the last Mughal emperor Bahadur Shah Zafar. Since then, the family has collected fine gemstones, jewellery and art, becoming experts in the intricacies of Indian art over the generations. Ghanshyam, like his father before him, is a connoisseur of Indian art collected from diverse regions, periods and religions.

"We never run out of inspiration," he says. "There is so much variety in our past. And of course we have the Taj Mahal itself, which was the inspiration for the Taj Signature Collection." Not that all inspiration comes from distant history. "My son Milind and I play golf, so we created a very successful golf-themed collection," he says. "We also created a collection based on Bharatanatyam, a classical Indian dance, using the shapes and elegance of the dancers."

The artistry and love of colour and pattern in Kohinoor's jewellery is expressed through gemstones of the highest quality. "Our jewellery is all about the stones, sapphires from Sri Lanka, for example, and rubies from Burma," says Ghanshyam. "We tend to buy stones in rough form and cut them to our specification." Often Kohinoor's jewellery begins not with a design but with the gemstones themselves, the design serving to enhance and display their particular qualities.

Fifth-generation Ruchira Mathur is Kohinoor's designer and works alongside her brother Milind Mathur, who is a graduate gemologist, certified by the Gemological Institute of America, and the company's Artistic Director. "They both have a flair for working with gemstones," says Ghanshyam, "It's in their blood." Ruchira and Milind bring a western sensibility to the jewellery collections, attuned to the tastes of the international visitors who come to Agra.

"Our jewellery is exposed to worldwide trends," says Ghanshyam. "Our customers demand the best quality and they know their jewellery. They immediately see that we offer very fine pieces." Each collection from Kohinoor Jewellers is one of a kind.

The company also offers a bespoke jewellery service, which is particularly suited to overseas visitors staying in Agra. The combination of stones and choice of settings are discussed and detailed design options created. The finished pieces are then shipped on completion.

Kohinoor Jewellers exactly defines what Ghanshyam calls "contemporary fusion": the perfect setting of expertly cut gemstones, reflecting the cultural and artistic traditions of India, and a stylish ability to bring these strands together in refined contemporary jewellery. "This fusion of modern, bespoke and heritage comes through in all our work," says Ghanshyam. As in-the-know visitors to Kohinoor Jewellers have discovered, the Taj Mahal isn't the only thing of beauty worth seeing in Agra.

www.kohinoorjewellers.com

SHINE OF THE TIMES

CROSSFOR

"We create products full of dreams," says Hidetaka Dobashi of his diamond jewellery company Crossfor Co Ltd. Dobashi's passion for gems has led him to invent new techniques with diamonds that produce jewellery with a difference.

Dobashi started his jewellery company in 1980 after studying at the Gemology Institute of America. Based in his home town of Yamanashi, Japan, the business really took off in 1999 when Dobashi came up with the "Crossfor cut" – a new way of cutting rough diamonds which avoids carving and thus damaging the stone.

"It is difficult to find well-cut diamonds," says Dobashi. "But after three years of intensive research, we succeeded in creating a cross-shaped cut in the centre of a jewel that achieves extra glitter with the reflection of light. Viewed from each side the reflection is a cross, but brilliance flashes from its 46 facets." The cut proved such a success that Dobashi has patented it globally in Japan and Britain. He has also had his designs patented in 12 countries including the USA and across Europe.

In 2010, a decade after this breakthrough, Dobashi invented a new diamond jewellery setting called the Dancing Stone. Unlike ordinary settings that use a laser hole to attach the stone to a stationary base, Dobashi's freer design means the slightest movement of the wearer causes movement in the gem. "It never stops glittering," says Dobashi. "The centre stone swings and flickers along with a person's heartbeat and breathing."

Dobashi, whose enthusiasm for diamonds is undimmed by the passage of time, describes the thinking behind his design for the Dancing Stone. "Diamond jewellery is the best because of its brilliancy," he says, "which is achieved by the reflection of light. So, I thought if the stone is always shaking then its brilliancy will shine like crazy, as if the jewellery is dancing. Hence the name." Four years after its launch, the setting received the Yamanashi Industrial Award (manufacturing). Swarowski has adopted it too, becoming an Ingredient Branding partner of Crossfor.

The design's many possibilities are fully showcased in Crossfor's three jewellery collections: Dancing Heart, Crossfor New York and Crossfor New York for Men. The collections are all made up of delicate designs inspired by things that shine in the natural world. Bright is a pendant inspired by the glitter of a shooting star. "Our Twinkle Tear earrings represent tears of joy overflowing from happiness and gratitude," says Dobashi. In the New York for Men collection the signature piece – Tribal Hook – is a pendant that carries the motif of a hook, a Japanese symbol of strength on the open sea.

Dobashi seeks to create designs that appeal to customers of all ages, cultures and genders. "We will keep producing jewellery whose creative beauty brings happiness to people all over the world," he says. The Dancing Stone is proving popular in Asia and America, with Europe Crossfor's next target market. Currently, Crossfor's Good Future designs, which feature the fan-shaped scroll motif of Suehirogari (a symbol of good luck in Japanese culture), are the company's bestsellers. "Chinese and Japanese people believe in fortune-telling and regard the future as something beautiful," says Dobashi. "So, I named this line of jewellery 'good future'." It's an apt name for the collection; and for a manufacturer designing his way to even more prosperous times.
www.crossfor.co.jp

Chapter Fourteen

DESIGNED FOR LIFE

ADDRESS TO IMPRESS

LAUREN BERGER COLLECTION

In the world of luxury travel, certain things are a given – lavish accommodation, extensive amenities, and excellent service. But, for Lauren Berger, the hospitality offered to guests of Lauren Berger Collection goes far beyond this. "Hospitality is really what I'm made of," she says. "This is not just my business, it's my life. If I only had a day to live, I'd spend that day taking care of my guests."

With around 300 select properties in more than 20 locations worldwide, Lauren prides herself on finding the perfect home for each guest; homes that are not only elegant and sophisticated but also the perfect fit for the guests staying there. "Hospitality is really what I am made of," she says. "It's not just what I do for a living. I take care and decorate for my guests to make them feel like they never left the comfort of their own home."

Lauren Berger Collection is underpinned by the philosophy of personalised hospitality, where a guest's every whim is fulfilled, and the team combines discretion with efficient service. A 20-hour day is not uncommon for New York-based Lauren, as she responds to emails and requests from guests from around the world, including Europe and Brazil. However, the most important thing is that individual touch. "I try to spend as much time as I can getting to know my guests before their arrival," she says. "Detailing in my homes is not just about comfortable beds, pillows, and blankets. It's about paying close attention to their needs, whatever they might be."

From the Hamptons to the Caribbean, from Paris to the Adriatic, the international properties offered by Lauren Berger Collection are spectacular. These include the magical vacation home in Westhampton Beach, New York (pictured, opposite, with Lauren Berger and her husband Dr Sidney Berger). One of the latest luxurious additions is Chalet des Sens in Megeve in the French Alps, whose unique quality, copious splendor, and unrivaled level of comfort make for an unforgettable stay and a devoted clientele.

"This outstanding chalet is truly one of a kind, with an appearance that's worthy of a piece of art," says Lauren. "A ski-in, ski-out chalet, it's one of the most extraordinary and most elegant homes in the world for rent. Its quality, location, and offering of a service so caring and respectful that it makes every guest feel like royalty mean there is no competition. We couldn't be more proud of our collaboration with the Chalet des Sens – a winter haven that's fit for a king."

Lauren Berger Collection offers membership programmes, while regular guests and those enjoying lengthy stays are rewarded with VIP Ambassador Concierge Service and the option to include yachts, luxury vehicles, and classic sports cars. No request is too difficult, be it private-jet services, a 24-hour butler, an in-house chef and sommelier, or a crew for a luxury yacht. "There's nothing I love more than taking care of my guests," says Lauren. "There are no limitations whatsoever, no boundaries. If it's legal, if it's possible, it's done."

The collection is expected to expand, enabling more guests to experience these outstanding levels of service and hospitality. "Some of the grandest families from around the world would like Lauren Berger Collection to represent their properties," says Lauren. "They own outstanding properties that have never been on the market."

Whether these properties belong to royalty or the tech elite, Lauren ensures every guest is given a welcome to prove the truth of her motto – "never leave home."

www.laurenbergercollection.com

MOTIVATIONAL SPEAKER

ESTELON

A small collection of battered old radios and stereos lies in a cabinet at the head office of luxury speaker manufacturer Estelon in Tallinn, Estonia. "This is the root of Estelon's history," says Alissa Vassilkova. "These belonged to our grandparents – they're how my father Alfred learnt where sound comes from. He opened them up and made them better as his love of music evolved into a curiosity for physics." They signify the start of a lifetime devoted to the dream of delivering perfect sound – a dream that led Alfred Vassilkov to found Estelon in April 2010.

Alfred Vassilkov, now 60, was born in St Petersburg and grew up surrounded by music. His father played the accordion at dances, his aunt taught piano and Alfred himself would tune into Radio Luxembourg to hear tinny renditions of his favourite Western pop songs. Soon his love of music and his inquisitive nature combined to take things in a new direction. "I wanted to understand how you could create sound from electricity," he says. "I began to take radios apart and adjust them to make them better."

After studying acoustics in St Petersburg, Alfred began to build speakers from scratch for himself and his friends, even making the speakers for his own wedding, although Soviet-era restrictions meant that materials were limited. In the early 1980s, he moved from St Petersburg to Estonia, where his mother had been born, and began designing speakers for a company that made radios. Alfred started to develop and deploy innovative techniques, not only to secure the best sound but also to make skilful use of scarce resources.

Following the collapse of the Soviet Union, Estelon faced competition from western technology giants. Alfred continued to experiment, but also visited international shows to see the latest in speaker technology and discover what consumers wanted and needed. He travelled with his daughters, Alissa and Kristiina, schooling them between shows on the science of sound. Both daughters, as well as their partners, are involved with Estelon. "We can support his ideas and bring them to the world," says Alissa. "We are helping his dream come true every day."

Alfred continued to develop his own speakers, working on a prototype for five years until he was ready to reveal it to the family. Over breakfast, they agreed to start a company and within six months the first Estelon speaker system was showcased in Denver in the US. It immediately drew acclaim thanks not only to its incredible sound quality but also to its striking appearance. "The speakers look amazing but their sculptural quality is crucial to their engineering," he says. "They are built from the inside out and the appearance creates the best conditions for all the components inside."

Awards soon followed, with Estelon continuing to push the boundaries with each new model. "The Extreme, our largest speaker system to date, contains a lifetime of experience and knowledge and can be adusted in rooms of different sizes," says Alfred. "Our latest model is the Lynx, which is wireless and features modular hardware that can be upgraded to account for the latest technological developments."

With a presence in more than 25 countries and a reputation for cutting-edge engineering, Estelon is growing in size and prominence. Through it all, Alfred has remained the pioneering spirit at its heart, drawing on decades of experience and his fascination with the physics of sound in his determination to trailblaze new frontiers.
estelon.com

REGAL ROOMS

LINLY DESIGNS

The brilliance of a crystal chandelier, the radiance of gold leaf and the tactile luxury of velvet and silk are best appreciated first-hand in a beautifully designed setting, furnished and accessorised with an interior designer's eye for detail. This is what draws clients from all across America to the Linly Designs showroom in Clarendon Hills outside Chicago. "There is nothing like it on the east or west coast," says Janet Linly, the company's President and CEO. "Our showroom is a masterpiece that presents the full range of design services we offer our clients."

The Clarendon Hills showroom covers 11,000 sq ft, with each carefully accessorised room an example of the refined, old-world European style that Linly Designs is known for. "Clients come in from LA, Texas and New York just to experience the showroom in person," says Linly. Bedrooms, kitchens, drawing rooms and dining rooms are furnished with warm, burnished woods, cut glass, swagged brocade curtains and richly patterned fine rugs.

"Regarding interiors, most of what you see in current trends is minimal and uninviting," says Linly. "I feel you need elements that make a house feel like home, that shows history and heritage. As we focus on regal and luxury

interiors, our design team always turns to top-quality artisans who produce classic and timeless designs." One such company is Fine Art Lamps, who supply many of the sophisticated lighting schemes in the Linly showroom.

In addition to the showroom and the full interior design service that it complements, a new invitation-only luxury website, bonnage.com, puts Linly's interiors clients in touch with a concierge service for high-end gifting. Janet Linly's success as an entrepreneur relies on her understanding of her clients' tastes. Now, Bonnâge curates gifts that show the same discerning eye for the unique and beautiful, whether a single piece or for hundreds of people.

"We offer sophisticated, personalised designs in lovely packaging," says Linly. "Our service makes clients feel special and their recipients feel special, too."

Bringing the high level of customer service that her clients receive from Linly Designs to bespoke corporate gifting through Bonnâge is also a way for Linly to extend the relationships she builds with her clients. "We want them to have something remarkable that reminds them of us," she says. "A customer relationship is really a people relationship."

www.linlydesigns.com · www.bonnage.com

OPTICAL ART

TELESCOPES OF VERMONT

A few years ago, Russ Schleipman found himself in the enviable situation of demonstrating a telescope to the Queen at the Chelsea Flower Show in London. But this was no ordinary telescope

It was a Porter Garden Telescope, a device first designed in 1920 and revived more recently by Russ's father, Fred (pictured, above). It is a stunning, Art Nouveau-style instrument that looks nothing like any other telescope. It acts as a sculpture and a sundial; but it also lets you see the rings of Saturn and the moons of Jupiter.

"It's a marriage of art and science," says Schleipman of Telescopes of Vermont, where these elegant, luxury devices are made to order. "People always ask what it is, because it looks like a long, leafy piece of botanical sculpture. Then you bring out a handsome leather case that holds the optics and it suddenly becomes a reflecting telescope. Point it at the sky and the moon fills the field."

It impressed not just the Queen but also Sir Patrick Moore, the late presenter of *The Sky At Night* and a man who did more than anybody else to promote astronomy in Britain. It was Moore who campaigned to have a crater on the moon named after Russell W Porter, the engineer and amateur astronomer who designed the original telescope and manufactured at least 55 of them in the 1920s and 1930s. The Smithsonian obtained one of these after it became a model for the gigantic Hale Telescope at the Mount Palomar Observatory in San Diego.

Engineer Fred Schleipman saw his first Porter Garden Telescope in a Vermont museum and was so captivated by it that he became determined to resurrect Porter's creation. It took several decades to persuade the museum to lend him its original telescope and allow replicas to be made, but the Schleipmans have now produced around 40, each retailing at $75,000. Each one takes four months to complete and requires the attention of a team of expert craftsmen who have painstakingly improved on Porter's model.

"The original design was genius but the execution was a little flawed," says Russ Schleipman. "We've also used sighting mechanisms to make it easier to find Jupiter and Saturn, which makes the experience much more pleasurable. All Porter's telescopes were slightly different as he was always improving the design, and I think he would approve of what we've done."

www.gardentelescopes.com

263

PALATIAL LUXURY

NORTHACRE

There aren't many people who can say the Queen is a neighbour – but residents of a new luxury development in St James's Park will be able to do just that. No.1 Palace Street, a historic property opposite Buckingham Palace, is being restored to its former splendour by luxury property developer Northacre.

The building has stunning views over the 42-acre gardens of Buckingham Palace, the only residential property in London able to make such a claim. Indeed, when Northacre's CEO Niccolò Barattieri di San Pietro was showing potential clients round the development the group saw a helicopter land in the palace grounds. Minutes later the Queen and her corgis stepped on to the lawn.

With 30 years of experience, Northacre prides itself on reviving architecturally significant buildings to create luxury residences in the capital's most sought-after locations, including The Lancasters in Hyde Park and The Phillimores in Kensington.

No.1 Palace Street is one of the company's most notable developments yet – an impressive island site on the edge of St James's Park that gives residents the chance to own a piece of history. Built in 1861, the property's Grade II-listed

Buckingham Gate was one of London's first landmark hotels and hosted some of Queen Victoria's most distinguished guests. The surrounding land had been a mulberry tree garden, an aviary for exotic birds in the reign of King James I, which is why the present-day protected enclave of Victorian buildings is now known as the Birdcage Walk Conservation Area.

No.1 Palace Street is a harmonious blend of five architectural styles, from 1880s French Beaux Arts to Contemporary, combining stunning interior architecture and sumptuous modern design. The development is due for completion in 2020 and comprises 72 luxury apartments with custom-designed interiors, many with 16 ft-high ceilings. The property has underground parking, a restaurant, a vast entertaining space, an elegant library, a 2,000 sq ft gym, personal training suites, treatment rooms, a spa and a spectacular 20 metre pool.

"Northacre has built more luxury homes than any other developer in London and this development will cement Northacre's position as an industry leader and set a new standard for what buyers demand from a home,"says Barattieri di San Pietro. "No.1 Palace Street is an exceptional proposition in an unrivalled location, and will tempt the most discerning of buyers."
www.northacre.com

Chapter Fifteen

A SENSE OF OCCASION

FOR COOL KIDS

ALEX AND ALEXA

Childrenswear is booming, as the influence of the Royal Family's youngest style icons Prince George, Princess Charlotte and now Prince Louis shows. Growth in kids' fashion has outstripped both men's and women's for the past five years, according to research firm Euromonitor. One reason is the rise of Alex and Alexa, the website that's been described as "the Net-a-Porter for under-14s".

The award-winning site – it has won *Junior* magazine's Best Online Fashion Retailer award four times since 2011 – sells an irresistible mix of luxury labels like Burberry, Gucci and Dolce & Gabbana, alongside more affordable high-street edits and cult brands from Spain and Scandinavia. It also has sportswear from Nike and Adidas, homewares, toys and gifts.

"The concept was to make busy parents' lives easier when shopping for their kids," says Commercial Director Rachele Hayman, who has been working in the kidswear industry for over 20 years. "We have everything they need in one place, making shopping quick and smooth." Hayman has seen how the shape of kidswear has changed with time, and has contributed her knowledge to the growth of the company.

The site was founded in London in 2008 by husband-and-wife team Alex Theophanous and Alexa Till, with the aim of bringing the world's best kids' brands together. In 2014, it was acquired by the Babyshop Group, owned by Marcus and Linn Tagesson, another husband-and-wife team. The couple had launched Babyshop.com, the website that brought Scandinavian labels like Mini Rodini to global prominence.

"Alex and Alexa was and still is, in my opinion, the number-one site within kidswear in Europe," says Marcus Tagesson. "The founders were branding geniuses and we want to remain pioneers." At Alex and Alexa fabulous party dresses sit next to stylish streetwear and innovative sports styles. Other popular brands include Bobo Choses and Stella McCartney. "Stella really gets kids," says Hayman. "She knows how to make fashion fun." McCartney's range for spring and summer 2018 is festooned with wonderful prints of donkeys, monsters, ice cream and seashells.

The site's buyers are invited to the headquarters of luxury labels such as Gucci in Milan to view the next season's collections. Social media is also a driving force and the company's Life & Style blog pulls in talented writers, photographers and tastemakers from around the world.

"We work closely with influencers such as Holly Willoughby, who does a brilliant job of representing us," says Hayman. "We also have a personal shopping service aimed at high-net-worth individuals, sports stars, royalty and the like. We show them the latest season's collections at their homes and help them find what they are looking for."

New brands are regularly introduced after careful vetting. "We go to the big fashion fairs and are always on the lookout for cool up-and-coming brands," says Hayman. "It's important that we can grow together and build them up after a few seasons."

The company supports the Wildhood Foundation, a Swedish organisation working to stop poaching and wildlife trading in Africa and Indonesia. "We are trying to give something back and we're doing that through the eyes of the future generation," says Tagesson.

For parents and children looking for coveted fashions, stylish sportswear and gorgeous gifts, all well made with high-quality design in mind, AlexandAlexa offers a stress-free shopping experience. What's not to love?
www.alexandalexa.com

BABY IT'S YOU

THE BABYSHOP GROUP

Over the past decade, Scandinavian kids' fashion brands have become known as some of the coolest on the planet. Colourful clothes by labels such as Mini Rodini and Bang Bang Copenhagen are coveted by parents for being as playful as they are practical, as sustainable as they are stylish. The man assisting the rise of Scandi fashion is 37-year-old Swedish entrepreneur – and father of two – Marcus Tagesson.

Tagesson and his wife Linn are the founders of Babyshop.com, the Stockholm-based site specialising in highly desirable designer baby clothes. When it was launched in 2006, Babyshop focused on small Scandinavian brands. It's now a one-stop shop for baby products that ships to more than 80 countries. "Ten years ago, labels like Mini Rodini were new and relatively unknown," says Tagesson. "We've definitely played a part in finding global reach for them."

Tagesson's championing of Scandi style has made him one of the most influential figures in children's fashion. After launching Babyshop, he acquired the London-based kids' designer fashion site Alex and Alexa in 2014. "The scope for Babyshop is limited, because of the name," he says. "Alex and Alexa can do the full range of clothes, toys and sportswear for children up to their teenage years. We hope it will allow us to become the global leader within the kids' space."

Other brands in the Babyshop Group include the Swedish kids' shop Oii and the homewares and toys company Lekmer. "We are opportunistic when we look at the market," says Tagesson. "We are definitely open to doing more acquisitions in the future."

Tagesson's rise from start-up entrepreneur to global player has been remarkable. He was born into a working-class family in Jönköping, Småland, the same province as

IKEA founder Ingvar Kamprad. Like Kamprad, Tagesson dreamed of owning his own business. "When I had the idea for Babyshop, I was studying to become a lawyer and considering a taking a finance course," he remembers. "Linn and I spotted a gap in the market when some friends had a baby and we couldn't find anywhere online to shop for them. We decided to start a house of brands for the busy parent."

The couple, who were just 24 and 25 at the time, rented a basement in Stockholm and spent every waking moment building their business. Babyshop soon became one of the premier online destinations for fashionable, functional baby gear, with stores in Sweden and Norway. Marcus and Linn now have two girls, age seven and five. "They have grown up with the business and love coming into the office and visiting during photo shoots."

Tagesson still runs The Babyshop Group from Stockholm. In London, Alex and Alexa is managed by Commercial Director Rachele Hayman. She joined the company after 25 years working at Arcadia Group as a Divisional Buying Director. Before that, she spent 11 years working at Marks & Spencer, building her knowledge of retail, fashion and buying around the world. "The vision is to become the worldwide leader in luxury kids' brands, with a great mix of price points and labels," she says. "We want to give customers the best choice in terms of stylish product."

For Tagesson, it's about selling clothes that are as good as they look. "Scandinavia has always been a world leader in responsible fashion that's both ecologically sound and ethically produced," he says. "I wouldn't sell anything I wouldn't dress my own kids in." Lucky kids.
www.babyshop.com

CRÈME DE LA CRÈME

JK7 SKINCARE

When Jurgen Klein, founder of skincare company Jurlique, sold his brand and moved with his wife, Karin, to Hawaii, to set up a luxury spa retreat, he was determined to leave the skincare market behind him.

"He was sick and tired of the lies people tell in the industry," says Karin. "But then he started to make his own spa products in the commercial kitchen, and they were wonderful. I challenged him to stop complaining and instead to create something better than what was available commercially. I said: 'Can you bring a product to market that is truly natural, organic and high performing with no chemicals at any stage of production?' He was hesitant – he's a biochemist and knows the difficulties – but he rose to the challenge."

And so, in 2015, after seven years of research and testing, JK7 was born. It is a pure, organic and anti-ageing, high-end skincare brand, handmade in tiny batches, using only the best natural ingredients and the most precious and expensive essential oils (including rose, myrrh and jasmine), powerful JK7 Signature Extracts and healing herbs. They are designed to improve the health of the skin, as well as its appearance.

In fact, university-commissioned research found that one star ingredient in JK7's signature extract, the rind of the mangosteen fruit, has anti-cancer properties, inhibiting malignant melanoma cells from spreading. The company can't, however, put this on the label because cosmetics are not classified as medicines.

"The abundance of herbal and natural ingredients in our products creates a synergy to help the skin function exactly as it's supposed to," says Karin. "We can't stop skin ageing – any cream that claims that is lying – but we can work against free radicals, preventing protein degeneration and accelerated ageing. We see skincare as one of the tools for a better, healthier holistic lifestyle. Our customers tend to be people who already have a high awareness of ecology and of their bodies, and who make conscious choices about the products they use. Kathy Freston, best-selling vegan author, is one of our fans."

The range is currently available for purchase in London, New York, Hawaii, Switzerland and Austria, from selected spas, hotels, high-end retail outlets and airport lounges, and is about to be launched in the Netherlands and Japan. Products can also be bought online via JK7's website. Future plans include an all-natural skin-whitening cream that works against age spots and discoloration as well as expansion into the Far East and Australia.

There are now 22 different products in the range, including face washes, serums and lotions. Given the purity and expense of the ingredients, the products are positioned at the very top end of the market, with the best-selling Serum Lotion – a luxurious day-and-night anti-ageing serum for all skin types – costing £1,415 for a 30 ml glass bottle.

"Our skincare is very exclusive and will never be for the mass market, or available everywhere," explains Karin. "That's because we took the decision not to compromise on quality or standards at any stage of the process. For example, each plant extraction takes about 50 hours with our spagyric extraction method that enhances the lifeforce of each healing plant, and every bottle is hand-sterilised, hand-filled and hand-packed. We have created something that is truthful, effective as well as luxurious. There is no comparison anywhere else on the market."

www.jk7skincare.com

RAIN OR SHINE

AQUASCUTUM

Aquascutum is famous for its unique blend of excellent quality and classic style. This quintessentially British brand has been at the cutting edge of craftsmanship and clothing design for well over a century, winning royal patronage, designing waterproof coats for First World War army officers and dressing Hollywood icons like Humphrey Bogart and Cary Grant.

"We are a brand that has been around for over 165 years and under new ownership we are investing in it and rebuilding it so that it will be around for at least the same again," says Philip Brassington, the company's Chief Operating Officer. "The heritage and DNA of the brand is about quality, innovation and modernity and these are areas we are focusing on."

Aquascutum was founded in 1851 by Mayfair tailor John Emary, who perfected the technique of treating wool fabrics to make them waterproof. Realising the significance of his rain-repellent cloth, he named the business Aquascutum – Latin for "water shield".

The company quickly flourished. The Prince of Wales, an arbiter of style who later became King Edward VII, was an early patron. The first royal client, he ordered a coat in Prince of Wales Check and in 1897 granted Aquascutum a royal warrant – the first of many.

During the First World War, Aquascutum supplied waterproof trench coats to army officers. In 1914, officers serving in the trenches had found that their standard issue coats were useless in atrocious conditions, so the company produced a heavy double-breasted coat, complete with epaulettes for securing binocular straps, a deep storm collar and cuff straps to stop water and mud getting up the sleeves.

After the war, the trench coats became part of civilian life and lightweight versions have been worn by men and women around the world ever since. Aquascutum also played a role in Edmund Hillary and Tenzing Norgay's historic ascent of Mount Everest in 1953, developing a hi-tech fabric to protect them against the extreme Himalayan weather.

In the intervening years Aquascutum has enhanced its reputation for innovation, creativity and top-flight design. A genuine luxury brand, it is a bastion of 21st century British style. "This is a very exciting time for Aquascutum," says Brassington. "In the coming year there will be a lot of activity, particularly around new product innovation, new store openings and new marketing campaigns – so expect to see a lot more of Aquascutum."

www.aquascutum.com

SOLE MATES

BALLY

When Bally Chief Executive Frédéric de Narp heard that the brand had been approached about a book celebrating the marriage of Prince Harry and Meghan Markle he immediately wanted the luxury footwear and accessories company to be part of it. "Prince Harry and Meghan Markle stand for inclusivity, progress, warmth and approachability," he says. "These are all values that we at Bally embrace. Harry and Meghan are not showy, but tasteful. They are young people who define the spirit of the age."

Bally is a company of deep heritage and youthful vigour, anchored in an exceptional heritage of shoemaking. Established in Switzerland in 1851, the brand's expertise has spanned fashion and practicality, simultaneously making products for sport, formalwear and streetwear alike. It produced the first designer sneakers in the 1930s, designed snow boots for the 1948 Winter Olympics, and created the mountaineering boots that took Sir Edmund Hillary and Tenzing Norgay to the summit of Mount Everest in 1953. In the 1980s Bally's trainers were even championed by hip hop pioneers including Doug E Fresh and Slick Rick.

For Frédéric de Narp, a 49-year-old father of seven, the royal couple fit in with Bally's historic aesthetic. "They are embracing the old and the new – bridging the gap between the two incredible countries of Britain and America," he says. "As a couple Harry and Meghan really embrace the entire world. You can really sense that joy everywhere, and the collective pride that the public hold in this couple and their marriage."

Championing exploration, discovery and sport, Bally's creative innovation and authenticity remains paramount today. Its unique design across shoes, accessories and ready-to-wear fashion is driven by a strong retro aesthetic inspired by the brand's rich archive. "As the world's most important luxury shoemaker, being associated with the Royal Family is both a privilege and an honour because, like them, we also defend tradition with a touch of modernity," says de Narp. For him, this union has captured the imagination of the public and is spreading a message of hope across the world.

"Their love also represents the adaptability of the monarchy in a way that has never before been displayed," says de Narp. "I think it is a unique and defining moment for Britain and for the world but also for the monarchy too. And Bally is delighted to be associated with it."
www.bally.com

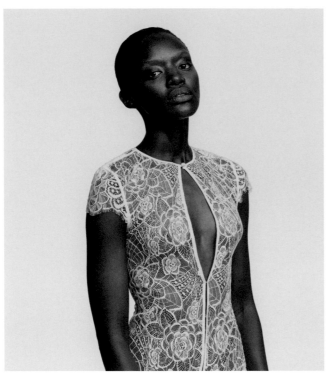
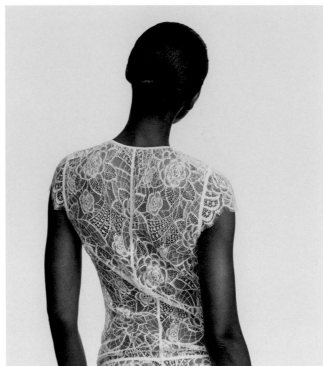

LICENCE TO THRILL

KIKI DE MONTPARNASSE

The New York-based luxury lingerie brand embodies the free spirit of its French namesake: Kiki de Montparnasse, an artists' model, literary muse and nightclub singer who turned heads in the Paris of the Roaring Twenties.

The brand sells lingerie-inspired ready-to-wear couture, including comfortable loungewear, swimwear, bridalwear and assorted accessories – much of it daring, sexy and provocative. It prides itself on creating pieces that help define and empower the modern woman.

"Our pieces appeal to those who are older who're still game or to someone who's younger who's comfortable with herself and is experimenting," says Jose Velasco Vega, Vice-President of Design and Production. "We really do have a range of customers and we're aspirational. We are not trying to infantilise women – our clothes are aimed at strong, independent women who have control of their lives."

What truly stands out is the quality of materials and the care taken during production. All-natural fabrics are imported from Europe while much of the brand's couture is handmade in New York.

"We have an atelier in our New York office," says Lindsay Fasso, Vice-President of Sales, "where we have

the ability to customise garments and give a one-of-a-kind, luxury experience."

The bridal collection features items that no bride should leave out of her trousseau. There are corsets and delicate bras to silk kimonos and a ruffle garter, or an ivory slip dress made from the softest cashmere. "Our design team is always looking for the next evolution of Kiki de Montparnasse," says Velasco Vega, "and they really have their finger on the pulse of what's happening in fashion."

A bestseller is the coquette bodysuit, which features a modern floral design and a keyhole opening. "It's one of the pieces that is part of the DNA of Kiki," says Fasso. "It hugs the body in all the right places. You can wear it indoors and out – a modern bride could wear that under a dress or as an accent. Or a partygoer could wear it out with jeans and a blazer. It speaks to a kind of versatility and elegance."

Modern women can find Kiki's delicate items in Harrods in the UK. "What we make is really about sensuality and about a woman's gaze," says Fasso. "It's all about how the woman herself is going to feel."
kikidm.com

CROWNING GLORY

PHILIP KINGSLEY

Philip Kingsley always understood that your hair can either be the greatest source of joy or an intense frustration. Inspired by the idea that every day should be a happy and healthy hair day, and with over 50 years of trichological expertise, Philip Kingsley created a range of award-winning treatments and scientifically formulated products to deliver just that.

From humble beginnings Philip Kingsley toiled hard to become a world leading authority on hair and was dubbed the "Hair Guru" by the international press. After qualifying as a trichologist in 1953, he opened his own clinic, developing a reputation for helping those with the most challenging hair and scalp concerns, and was soon attracting supermodels, celebrities and royalty.

"Our best-selling product is the Elasticizer which was created for Audrey Hepburn," says Anabel, daughter of Philip and a qualified trichologist herself. "Her hair was constantly damaged on set. Elasticizer was the world's first pre-shampoo treatment, nourishing hair without weighing it down." Other pioneering projects include the Flaky/Itchy Scalp Shampoo, and the breakthrough Trichotherapy 3-step regime for fine and thinning hair – which the team of trichologists spent more than seven years perfecting. Today, Philip Kingsley has become the go-to brand for stars such as Gwyneth Paltrow, Cate Blanchett and Victoria Beckham.

Now with a flagship clinic in Mayfair and another in New York City, the Philip Kingsley brand has become synonymous with trichology, the science of the hair and scalp. "We treat the most challenging types of hair and scalp concerns," says Anabel. "Our holistic approach not only investigates what products and styling rituals a client uses, but also delves into general wellbeing, medicines, and nutritional deficiencies. It was my father who discovered the importance of scalp health. Healthy, beautiful hair starts with a healthy scalp". Today Philip Kingsley has developed a range of award-winning products based on decades of exceptional trichological expertise. This not only includes an array of hair texture-targeted shampoos, conditioners and styling products, but also nutritional supplements for optimum hair and scalp health from within.

It is this product perfection, mixed with the compassionate and emphathetic nature of the trichologist consultation, which makes Philip Kingsley the go-to brand for happy, healthy hair. "We are helping everyone achieve their best head of hair," says Anabel. "We are proud to make a real difference in people's lives." *www.philipkingsley.co.uk*

HEAVEN SCENT

MILLER HARRIS

"London has always been known as a hothouse for contemporary art, culture and creativity," says Matthew Huband, Marketing Director at the luxury perfumer, Miller Harris. "We represent this dynamism and creativity through our inspirational fragrances, candles and body products."

Established by British master perfumer Lyn Harris in 2000 and with many of her original creations still available, the brand is now making exciting strides into the future, taking a contemporary approach to traditional perfume creation. Miller Harris looks for inspiration in the unexpected juxtapositions of the city. "Just as London sends tendrils out into nature, so nature can be discovered on hidden rooftops, in green parks and pushing up through the concrete," says Huband. "This is the core of Miller Harris."

As well as creating unique stories through the perfume itself, the experience of being in a Miller Harris store is unlike any other. Multi-disciplinary art-forms are given space to describe the perfumes in a series of collaborations. Specially commissioned soundscapes can be heard next to individual perfumes and colour, texture and bespoke materials illustrate the scents. Each store has a different "muse" which allows the space to work as more than just a shop. For instance,

the recently opened store at Canary Wharf (called The Artist) features a huge wall where contemporary artists are exhibited. At the Westfield store (The Poet), stacks of paperback books support the precious perfumes and regular poetry readings can be enjoyed with a glass of fizz.

Miller Harris staff are recognised as experts in perfume. "They are incredibly knowledgeable, empowered and key to the customer experience," says Huband. "Describing perfume through words is as difficult as talking about music, or trying to explain how silk feels, so we try to interpret the fragrances through different senses, to create experiences through sound, touch, visual representation or even poetry. Our experts describe the inspirations behind each perfume and the fragrance notes in a way that personalises each scent. In this way we hope to create real connections with our customers. It's about stories, not stores; productions not products."

A truly British company, Miller Harris embraces the beauty in the unconventional and the wonder in the ordinary, just like their home city. London is a melting pot of creativity and diverse stimuli, Miller Harris reflect that through scent, telling contemporary urban stories for modern bohemians.
www.millerharris.com

Chapter Sixteen

THE ART OF ENJOYMENT

———

ALL BETS ARE ON

PADDY POWER

"We're not your average bookmaker," says Paddy Power, with a conspiratorial grin. "We've built our brand on good humour, Irish charm, and a healthy sense of mischief."

The company's personality seems to radiate from Paddy, who has the same name as the firm that his father co-founded. Paddy is the grandson of Richard Power, who established his original bookmakers as an on-track stand at the races in Waterford, 1895. Then in the 1980s, faced with a deluge of British bookies as a result of tax regulation changes, a holy trinity of Irish bookmakers – Stewart Kenny, John Corcoran and Paddy's father David Power – joined forces to take on the English invasion.

"Bookmaking has changed a lot since the days of horseracing and tote boards," says Paddy. "Paddy Power was the first to introduce betting on non-sporting events, such as 'who will be the next prime minister?' or 'when will Harry and Meghan get engaged?'"

This so-called "novelty betting" has been a game-changer for Paddy Power: it's what's sets the firm apart and helped it to grow rapidly. People can bet on pretty much anything these days, says Paddy – from the results of *Love Island* to the weather. You can even bet on the end of the world this year (though it's unclear how you'd claim your winnings).

"Novelty betting can be risky," Paddy admits, "but that's what makes it good fun. For example, when Donald Trump first emerged as a presidential candidate, everyone thought it was a joke and his odds were around 200/1. Obviously, you know the story – he went on to get elected and we lost about £4 million as a result. So then we introduced a few novelty bets around his inauguration: will the crowd be smaller than Obama's? What colour tie will he wear? How often will he say his various catchphrases? And the interest was overwhelming.

Now we have a website dedicated exclusively to Donald Trump-related bets, and slowly but surely we're making back our losses. We even hired a Head of Trump Betting last year! That's how serious the demand has been."

Of course, playing the part of the lovable antagonist isn't without its controversy. Paddy Power's inherent sense of mischief can sometimes land them in hot water, but he enjoys causing a stir. "It's about poking fun at the right targets," he says. "During the 2015 marriage-equality referendum in Ireland, we released an advert with the slogan 'Tiocfaidh Ár Lá' (our day will come) accompanied by an image of two men in balaclavas kissing, and the odds on the result of the referendum vote. The slogan has traditionally been associated with the IRA, so it was a provocative statement to make in Ireland: it was a brave thing to do and it could have backfired, but we pride ourselves on being mischievous and sharp-witted but ultimately on the right side."

One of Paddy Power's most memorable stunts came in the Euro 2012 football tournament, when Danish forward Nicklas Bendtner flashed a pair of the brand's "lucky pants" after scoring (pictured, opposite). "Only a handful of people knew it was coming – he'd forgotten to do it after his first goal, so we thought it wasn't happening." Bendtner was fined £80,000 by governing body UEFA, sparking more controversy as, a day later, racist chanting by Croatian supporters received a lesser fine. "UEFA gave the stunt a second wind of publicity – how could it possibly be worse than racist chanting? Madness."

"Most people understand our fun and mischief in the humour it's intended," Paddy shrugs with a smile. "At the end of the day, it's all good craic."
www.paddypower.com

LATIN LESSONS

ARTE AL LÍMITE (AAL)

"Ana María is a very important art collector here in Chile," says Elisa Massardo, editor of the art magazine *Arte Al Límite* (AAL), of its founder Ana Maria Matthei. "She ran a successful gallery for many years before realising, through her regular attendance at art fairs and exhibitions, that catalogues are the most effective and visual way to circulate artists' work."

On launching AAL in 2001, Matthei's vision was for a contemporary art magazine which would make a valuable contribution to culture and showcase Latin American art on the international stage. AAL is now a bi-monthly collection magazine that is one of the most influential art publications in Latin America. It prints 8,000 copies of each issue, featuring outstanding artwork and exclusive interviews with artists from around the world, particularly those from Latin America.

"Our collection was designed to highlight and democratise art," says Matthei. "The aim is to encourage creation and demonstrate that it is possible to be an artist, that the world can indeed be observed from a single room."

Arte Al Límite attends around 40 international art fairs each year – including those in the UK, Italy, Spain, Switzerland, Hong Kong, the UAE and Latin America – searching for something special among the crowds of promising new talent.

"Almost every new artist we discover is someone we have met at a fair or exhibition," says Massardo. "Journalists, art critics and curators also send us their recommendations for artists they think we should feature. Typically, we'll publish four or six well-known artists plus a couple of new artists per issue."

"The artwork we feature needs to be original and innovative," says Matthei. "It needs to have real personality and captivate our imaginations. It also needs to be very visual to work in that medium."

To complement the flagship magazine, now in its 17th year and its 90th eddition, AAL's website is an important showcase of artists' portfolios. AAL has also published more than 15 luxurious art books, showcasing the traditions and innovations of the continent. These include titles on Chilean urban culture, contemporary Peruvian art and Fibras Latinoamericanas (Latin American Fibres), featuring 40 emerging female artists from Central and South America and the Caribbean.

"We hope very soon to have our own exhibition space for AAL and to hold exhibitions in the cultural centres of Chile and Latin America," adds Matthei. "Then perhaps we will achieve our goal of making art accessible for everyone."
www.arteallimite.com/en

APPENDICES

INDEX

CREDITS

PUBLISHER

St James's House
298 Regents Park Road
London N3 2SZ

Phone: +44 (0)20 8371 4000
publishing@stjamess.org
www.stjamess.org

Richard Freed, Chief Executive
richard.freed@stjamess.org

Stephen van der Merwe, Managing Director
stephen.vdm@stjamess.org

Richard Golbourne, Sales Director
r.golbourne@stjamess.org

Ben Duffy, Communications Director
ben.duffy@stjamess.org

Stephen Mitchell, Head of Editorial
stephen.mitchell@stjamess.org

Aniela Gil, Senior Designer
aniela.gil@stjamess.org

John Lewis, Deputy Editor
john.lewis@stjamess.org

Photography
Nunn Syndication, Getty Images. Other images
are the copyright of individual organisations.